Also by Norman S. Pratt

NOBLE CONFLICT
A Vietnam War Novel

Published in 2005
By
iUniverse
iuniverse.com

PEARLS

for the

MOMENT

THINGS WE SHOULD HAVE LEARNED A LONG TIME AGO

Norman S. Pratt

iUniverse, Inc.
Bloomington

Pearls for the Moment
Things We Should Have Learned a Long Time Ago

iUniverse books may be ordered through booksellers or by contacting:

iUniverse
1663 Liberty Drive
Bloomington, IN 47403
www.iuniverse.com
1-800-Authors (1-800-288-4677)

ISBN: 978-1-4502-6604-8 (pbk)
ISBN: 978-1-4502-6603-1 (cloth)
ISBN: 978-1-4502-6605-5 (ebk)

Printed in the United States of America

iUniverse rev. date: 12/27/2010

To my grandchildren:
Daniel, Julia, Jessica, Alexander, and Rebecca

Contents

I – INTRODUCTION

Pearls for the Moment is about the many little things we should have learned a long time ago, things we knew but never understood, things we forgot, and things we need to know before we need them.

It is also about personal goals, interpersonal relationships, and happiness. It is written for those with little or no formal training in philosophy, the sciences, or the social sciences.

It is also, in part, a personal journal about my observations on life's mysteries and my own opinions about life. In addition, it is a factual publication, meant to provide a simple explanation of useful but often misunderstood theories and concepts.

Hopefully you will glean an appreciation for some elements of personal philosophy—how we live our lives, how we meet life's challenges, how we cope with stress; in other words, how we find happiness in living. In that regard, some technical background information, not normally considered when developing a personal philosophy but often needed in life, is included. Hopefully you will find most of the data presented herein simple and well organized. Thus, it is easy to find what you are looking for when you need it; and when you find it, it is readily understandable.

Pearls for the Moment is about personal philosophy and self-improvement. It is a book about science, faith, opinion, and yes, esoteric (secret) subjects, as well as daily life essentials. Not everyone will understand everything in it. Not everything in it will be correct. Some of it is just my personal opinion. That's okay. It is supposed to leave you with the desire to learn more and to think more about personal philosophy; it is to be used on occasion as a *Self-Help Guide to Personal Philosophy*.

Some may question how I could possibly have the arrogance and audacity to write this book. Believe me, I have no more knowledge or wisdom than anybody else. I just like to study and write. I wrote it as a lifelong learner who is interested in social, scientific, and economic theories and concepts. The subjects covered in this book were learned through high school and college schooling, a lot of reading, and lots of experience—just like you must learn. This is a book about facts, opinions, and faith.

To the best of my knowledge and understanding, the facts contained here are reasonably accurate. If any are not, please feel free to contact me at the e-mail address noted on the last page of the discussion questions. The opinions herein are mine, just like your opinions are yours. If you disagree with my opinions, you may also feel free to contact me.

I wrote this book because I had something to say. I am not formally trained as a writer. I learned to write by reading and writing for a long time, and working with some very good editors. I was trained as an engineer. As such, it has been difficult for me to assimilate and put in writing all the ideas I want to express—or for that matter, to even understand them. I was not trained to properly express myself to anybody—not my boss, not my peers, not my clients, not competitors. I was not even trained to deal with my wife, the love of my life. As far as the social sciences are concerned, I was really stupid.

I was so stupid that it cost me much happiness and much freedom. Maybe I tried to do too much. I always tried to balance my job with my career and with my family. Did I bat zero? Nearly, but thanks to my technical training, I always had a job. Thanks to my wife, I always had a family.

When I was beginning my professional career as a freshman in college, my father gave me advice I followed the rest of my life: "Go as fast as you can and see what happens." That was good advice to an eighteen-year-old teenager who at the time was afraid he was going to flunk out of engineering school. Dad knew I lacked the confidence of experience and gave me the best advice he had for the moment. I took it. For the next four years, I went as fast as I could. I worked long hours. Gradually things improved. I learned how to study. I learned how to take tests. I learned how to enjoy learning.

After college, I tried to continue to follow Dad's advice, "Go as fast as you can and see what happens." But for some unknown reason, what happened was not always to my liking. Even so, that was the only way I knew.

That's the way many of us approach our lives—our personal lives, our public lives, and our professional lives. Crash ahead full speed toward what we hope will be a fruitful, productive, and happy life working in a profession we love—one that will bring us wealth, honor, and satisfaction in our public life; peace, security, and love in our private life; and every so often, immediate gratification.

For those of us who live long enough, there comes a time to look back and ask, "What happened? Why did we do it that way? What should we have done? What should we do next?"

Chances are many of us never give much thought to everyday decisions. We just do what we are trained to do. We do, however, often pay attention to the many important decisions we make. We may rationalize, "Whatever happens, happens." We may ask "Why?" We may ask, "Do the decisions we make really make a difference in our lives?" or is it like Forrest Gump's mother who says, "Life is like a box of chocolates. You never know what you're going to get next." Well, at least Forrest knew that when he opened that box, those little brown things were chocolates.

When we choose a career, we know generally what we want to do. We will be an engineer, a lawyer, a doctor, a carpenter, a truck driver, a civil servant, or whatever. In making our career decisions, however, we also must consider lifestyle. We might love the work but hate the lifestyle, yet we choose a career and then head in that direction. Chances are *the direction we head in is probably where we will end up.*

Those who take liberal arts often look back and find they are lacking in technical understanding and have no immediately marketable skills. Those who pursue technical careers often look back and find they are lacking in social and political skills. Many of us are socially and politically inept. I certainly am. Social and political skills are foreign to my nature. I was never formally trained to deal with people. I was trained as an engineer. I spent years in school laboring over math and science. In college I studied no history, no philosophy, no psychology, and only one year of English. I went out into the professional world well-trained to provide an employer with professional skills. I was marketable. I was trained to meet technical needs. I was trained to deal with things structural, things mechanical, and things electrical. But I was not trained to deal with people.

Many of us have few or no social or political skills. Even so, most of us manage to interact with others pretty well under circumstances we can control, but how about under circumstances over which we have little or no control?

Fortunately, or unfortunately, we live in two worlds: a private world of family and friends, and a public world where we work to make a living and interact in the public realm. Our private world is supposed to be a world of love and comfort with the basic laws of nature watched over by God. The public world is different. The public world is a world of man-made laws watched over by an army of lawyers and politicians. In both worlds, we frequently encounter stress.

Too often, we lack training in the business of how to handle stress. That lack of training sometimes takes a heavy emotional toll in our lives. We all develop different ways to deal with the stress. Some of us exercise. Some read. Some turn to religion. But in one way or another, all of us develop our own personal philosophy about how to handle stress.

We develop our philosophy, wittingly or unwittingly, through studying, observations, and participation in life—some good, some not so good. We search for and find moral guidance from our parents, from church, from our teachers, from friends and mentors, and from our personal experiences. Our personal philosophy changes throughout our lives.

Christians put their trust in the Holy Bible for basic moral values. They try to follow biblical teachings and nature's absolute rules. But in what do they put their trust in their public and professional lives? Do they simply try to live pure lives, and when moral dilemmas come up, "Put it in God's hands"? Do they simply ask forgiveness for personal sins while looking the other way at public and professional moral dilemmas by responding with, "Leave unto Caesar that which is Caesar's and unto God that which is God's"?

Too often, those approaches lead to moral dilemmas that affect not only our professional lives, but our private and public lives as well. To resolve moral dilemmas, many of us turn to religion; others of us turn to philosophy. I turned to both. I read and studied the Bible. I read and studied books of the great philosophers. In the end, I became so overwhelmed that my brain couldn't handle all the wisdom of the ages. Finally, I thought, there must be a better way than reading all this stuff.

I became determined to try to simplify the profundity of academic intellects by putting the complex into a brief clear format that could be easily referenced and understood at the practical level. So I wrote this book. I wrote it not to fill up pages with any liberal or conservative prejudices or with any specific answers to specific problems. Rather it is written to help you appreciate the basics of life and to arrange your thoughts on personal philosophy.

Along the way, I interject some of my own personal experiences. I do this not because you will be interested in my background, but because it may help you to recognize in your own life, and in the lives of others, the importance of the moment. Also, this is not a textbook; this is a book about basics. For simplicity, some of the numerical values quoted herein are orders of magnitude values rather than exact values.

It is intended for this book to be first read in its entirety, but slowly, one chapter at a time. There is no particular order of reading. You may read or skip whatever chapters you want. It is my hope that you can use *Pearls for the Moment* to help you define your own personal philosophy—and to give you a little advantage over the turkeys with whom you have to fly.

2 – THE MOMENT

Hundreds, if not thousands, of poems, songs, books, plays, movies, and sayings have in their title the word *moment*. Moment is a word of meaning. It can mean now, such as this moment; it can mean then, such as that moment; or it can refer to significant periods of time, such as great moments in history. In any case, moment refers to a time of special importance—an unusual time held in esteem.

A moment is usually thought of as very short duration. In medieval times, it was one and one half minutes. Sometimes it is only an instant, such as the moment I passed out in Vietnam when a sniper's bullet buzzed overhead. Sometimes it is a few seconds, such as love at first sight, like when I fell in love with my wife when first seeing her step off a school bus at college band camp. Or it can be a longer time, such as the high school football game in which I had six passes intercepted. It may be a moment of splendor, as in college when, as ROTC battalion commander, I turned toward a formation of six hundred uniformed and armed soldiers and yelled, "Battalion." The company commanders yelled over their shoulders the word, "Company." And then I yelled out the order of execution, "Present arms," and six hundred men brought their M1 rifles to a rifle salute. That was great. For me, that brought a feeling of power and honor.

Moments are personal. They play on a specific stage. All moments are fleeting. They pass quickly and cannot be relived. But they remain in our memory, especially when accompanied by strong emotion. We tend to remember things that are important to us. Memory affects the rest of our lives. Memory affects our every action, our every decision, and our happiness or unhappiness. That is why every moment is so important. That is why we must treat every moment with care.

Some moments we are prepared to deal with. Some moments we are not prepared to deal with. The moments we are prepared to deal with, we relish because we are in control; we can control the outcome to satisfy our comfort level. But moments we are not prepared to deal with cause us anguish. We are at the mercy of others. Moments like when a schoolchild brings home a failing report card, or a teenager gets caught by the police for underage drinking, or an adult loses a job or must endure the loss of a child. It is in moments of failure, in moments of defeat, in moments of loss that we need the most help.

In good times, we simply enjoy the moment. In bad times, we get in touch with our souls, and we get in touch with God; we draw upon the wisdom of the universe.

The moment is what we make it, our perception of what we sense, what we see, hear, feel, touch, and smell. Unfortunately, it is also what we glean from cynics, those sneering and sarcastic people who believe human actions are insincere and motivated by self-interest; and from competitors, those who seek to defeat us; and from those who covet, those who have a strong desire to have what belongs to others; and from overzealous TV journalists, those careless and sometimes insincere talking heads who get paid lots of money to upset us for little reason.

Each moment is important. Like the Church Lady says, "Isn't that special?" We may laugh at statements like that; we may find them below our intellectual level, or we may embrace the realization that each moment is "special" no matter what we are doing. As so elegantly expressed in Ecclesiastes, *"There is a right time for everything"* and "There is nothing better for a man than to be happy and to enjoy himself as long as he can."

We may not remember much about routine moments that happened just yesterday, but we can remember in great detail significant moments that happened many years ago—especially moments accompanied by strong emotion. It is astounding how much we remember about those moments that make a significant impact on us. They are moments we may recall unwittingly. When the conscious memories of past moments recalled are good, relish them. *When the conscious memories of past moments recalled are bad, let them come out anyway. Don't suppress them. Relax; give them time to play out. They will disappear.* Refuse to let bad moments last; and if you want to maintain your sanity, don't dwell on them.

God intended each moment to be special and to be savored and enjoyed unhurriedly. Each moment is sacred in that it is the manifestation of our God-given powers to make our own decisions, to set our own path, to interact with other persons, and to interact with our environment. Each moment is a time to participate. Each moment is a time to learn. Each moment is a time to draw upon our memories of the past and to prepare our minds and souls for the future. Whenever, whatever, all moments are yours.

These moments, good and bad, call for and sometimes demand from us a response. It may be a response to an event, or to a member of our family, a coworker, a friend, or an enemy. This book is intended to help you recognize how to properly respond to such moments. This book is intended to help you not miss the forest for the trees, while at the same time maintaining the ability to hone in on a specific tree—to see at one glance both the big picture and the important details.

I have included in this book a few pearls that I wish I had known before I needed them. Some of these pearls I once knew but had forgotten. Many I never knew. I have written some of them down here for easy reference; to do that, I found it necessary to sometimes break the time-honored rule against the use of worn-out phrases, like I've already done several times. Those of you still reading know that is what this book is about. It is about those many little time-honored phases and facts we never knew or we forgot. It is to help us to learn, review, remember, and find important little pearls of knowledge at exactly the right moment. That is why you are reading it. That's why I wrote it. I did it for me. I did it for you. This is my little contribution to the hundreds of writings about the moment. Recognizing the relative importance of any moment, and knowing how to deal with it, is just part of the basics.

3 – BASICS

Have you ever walked into a meeting in the middle of a discussion on a seemingly complex topic with which you are unfamiliar? If you have, you must know the helpless feeling of trying to understand what is going on without having adequate background information. If you sit there and listen long enough, you may glean enough information to recognize what the actors are talking about. You may pick up a few interesting facts to appreciate the subject matter. But you will never truly understand the subject until you understand the basics.

Basics are important elementary facts and assumptions about a given subject or topic. They are usually phrased in simple, easy-to-understand terms, without any fancy confusing twitches. *Fundamentals (facts)* and *principles (assumptions)* serve as the basic starting point and retain their integrity throughout when problems are encountered at more advanced or complex stages.

Basics are simple, undisputable elements of logic. They must be sound. Sound fundamentals and principles must always apply; they never change. They are normally easily understood by both professionals and laymen.

No matter what we are doing, how we are doing it, or at what stage we are doing it, to be successful we must always follow the basics. We must always be guided by sound fundamentals and principles. We must study, learn, and remember the basics to avoid unnecessary confusion and to be successful. And we must always be able to maintain our bearings, even when things become overly complex and misleading.

For most of us, it is simply impossible to remember all the basics. Occasionally we need to review them to determine if they are still sound, or to learn anew, or to determine which apply at the moment. Often, we may discover conflicting principles, such as liberal and conservative views.

Conflicting principles lead to conflict. Conflicting principles cannot coexist. You must chose one and abandon the other. Choose you must.

Keep it simple. My cousin, a librarian, once told me that whenever she researches a new subject, she always looks for a sixth-grade book to start with. Books written at the sixth-grade level are usually accurate, simple, and easily understood. Nowadays, of course, you also have the Internet. But no matter what you use to learn the basics, keep it accurate and keep it simple.

4 – PHILOSOPHY

Is your philosophy of life sound? Do you even know what philosophy means?

Philosophy is an attitude, *a way of thinking*—a way of thinking about the basic concepts of life, such as religion, truth, right behavior, science, and politics.

Philosophy is a recognized discipline that examines basic concepts such as existence, cause, and freedom. It also represents the academic study of life, of nature and reality. It is given to thinking about the larger issues and deeper meanings of life. It refers to guiding underlying principles of a specific sphere of knowledge, of a particular school of thought, or to a set of beliefs or aims, be they right or wrong, fair or unfair.

Like it or not, we must all develop our own personal philosophy of life. No one else can do that for us. We may be influenced by our mother, our father, our pastor, our teachers, our mentors, our coworkers, our bosses, and our political leaders; but in the end, we must each develop our own personal philosophy.

That development usually begins at home, where we learn the value of love and nurturing. Then comes school, where we begin to accumulate knowledge. But school also instills in us, for better or worse, competitiveness—a competitiveness we need to survive in a competitive world; to provide our families with food, shelter, and clothing; and to meet our emotional needs for power, fame, glory, and honor. But after all of this, after meeting our physical needs, after the fame, glory, and honor, many of us eventually find that true happiness is not where we look for it; rather, it is found in knowledge and understanding.

Traditionally, philosophy has been mostly for the old because they have the time for it. The young are too busy to partake of its beauty—too busy studying to learn the basic skills for survival, too busy working and making a living, and too busy playing in order to recover from the stresses of life in this demanding world. Most people are simply too busy to read and assimilate works of the great masters. Most people simply watch TV to relieve stress and bring them temporary happiness. But people of all ages can find the joys of philosophy in learning, in understanding.

The word *philosophy* is derived from the Greek word meaning *lover of wisdom*. True philosophy discovers the joy of learning, the joy of understanding. Man is a bundle of changing perceptions; he needs to know his perceptions to be accurate and true. To know that, man needs knowledge and understanding of that knowledge.

Classical philosophy refers to the ways of thinking developed over many years by great thinkers, including the early Greeks, early religious leaders, the great rationalists (with views appealing to reason), the great empiricists (who held the theory that knowledge is derived from experience), the idealists, and others.

Socrates and his student *Plato* were the founders of moral philosophy. They taught the values of morality and justice. Plato's student *Aristotle* believed and taught that the soul is at the core of being; it is the first activity of the living body, and humans have bodies for rational activity. Aristotle recognized that man is a political animal; he depends on, must interact with, and must resolve conflicts with his fellow man.

Saint Augustine fused Platonism with Christianity. *Copernicus* and *Newton* unveiled the universe. These great men gave us the basic guidelines we still follow today.

Then there are the likes of *Machiavelli*. Machiavelli, for better or worse, studied and wrote about politics and government as actually practiced. Machiavelli is still read today by most students of politics and business, as well as entrepreneurs. Machiavelli's honest descriptions of what really goes on in politics are shocking. His pragmatic teachings still give us insight into life in today's world, where we sometimes have to swim with the sharks.

By *contemporary philosophy*, I mean, "What's happening now?" Well, that depends on your perspective: the perspective of the American Philosophical Society or that of the rest of us. The American Philosophical Society is a scholarly organization of international reputation that promotes useful knowledge in the sciences and humanities through excellence in scholarly research, professional meetings, publications, library resources, and community outreach. It lists more than thirty categories of membership under mathematics and physical sciences, biological sciences, social sciences, humanities, and the arts. Today there are about one thousand members. Each year the society elects about forty new members, mostly prestigious college professors, successful researchers, and well-known statesmen. The society supports research and serves scholars.

But vast numbers of people receive their philosophical input data from popular self-help books on the market today: books on subjects ranging from quantum physics to the power of the subconscious mind, from politics to happiness. The most popular publications are those written in simple, easy-to-understand terms.

Paraphrased quotations from several philosophers are included as an appendix to this book. I hope some of these paraphrased quotations arouse your interest enough for you to read some of these publications and to develop and think about your own personal philosophy.

Personal philosophy is a personal attitude—the qualities that make each of us different and distinct from all others, our personal set of values, our personal standard of belief and behavior. Each of us must continually develop our own personal philosophy. In a continually changing world, our personal philosophies must also change. We must stay current, or we will be left behind. Staying current demands time, a commodity many of us don't have. I hope, for some of you at least, this book places at your fingertips a few basic things you need to help evaluate and revise your own personal philosophy.

5 – MEANING

Have you ever listened to someone talk and understood what they were talking about, but misinterpreted the meaning of what they said? You may have been the victim of *multiplicity of meaning*. Even simple words like *work* and *politics* have multiple meanings.

The word *work* has over thirty separate and distinct meanings. Work may mean such things as a paid job, an artistic or intellectual composition, to be successful, or a means of energy transfer. The word *politics* may refer to activities associated with government, or it may refer to power relationships among people, groups, or organizations.

Have you ever listened to someone talk and understood what they were talking about, but had no idea what they meant? I once had that problem with the simple word *function*.

Dumb as it may seem, I spent the first several weeks of college calculus wondering what the professor meant by the word *function*. The word *function* has over ten separate and distinct meanings. Our calculus professor lectured to a group of several hundred freshmen. He used many terms with which some of us were unfamiliar. He used common terms in a mathematical way without ever explaining what the terms meant. I guess he assumed we already knew what *function* meant. I did not. Well, come to find out, in mathematics, *function* means a variable quantity whose value depends upon the varying values of other variable quantities, or x = y, where x is a function of y. In calculus, the term is f(y) = y, or the function of y equals y. The confusing terminology is ridiculous.

Have you ever listened to someone talk and had no idea what they were even talking about? It's usually very easy to understand. You just need to know the jargon.

Every discipline has its own jargon. Neuroscientists refer to physical locations in the brain as prosencephalon instead of forebrain and rhombencephalon instead of rear brain. Engineers refer to words like electromagnetic radiation, section modulus, and entropy—buzz words usually understood only by trained professionals. The basics of these terms are quite simple.

Electromagnetic radiation is simply self-propagating energy waves, with electric and magnetic components oscillating at right angles to each other. They travel through space at the speed of light. They travel forever, until they give up their energy to something else, like radiant heat. It is this natural gift of electromagnetic radiation that transfers energy through space.

Section modulus is a simple structural engineering term referring to the property of any given section that, when divided into the applied bending moment (like breaking a pencil), produces the maximum stress at the extreme fiber of the given shaped section, assuming straight line stress distribution from the neutral axis (point of zero stress).

Entropy is a thermodynamic term that is a measure of the energy within a system that is unavailable to do work. For example, when considering the universe as the defined system, the entropy of the sun is enormous. If the unavailable energy of the sun could only be harnessed, there would never be an energy crisis, ever. Every system has energy. The key is to be able to capture that energy, or to reduce the entropy, to reduce the energy within the system that is unavailable to do work.

Many drug names are rhythmic cacophony of unpronounceable syllables. The result is that the average consumer knows little or nothing about the drugs he is taking. To better understand drugs and chemistry, you would need the *Compendium of Chemical Terminology*, the *Compendium of Analytical Nomenclature, Quantities, Units and Symbols in Physical Chemistry*, and other references published by the International Union of Pure and Applied Chemistry.

Every drug has three names: chemical, generic (nonproprietary), and brand (proprietary). Believe it or not, there are marketing consulting firms developing marketable drug names. Naming strategies include unique names that sound high tech, instead of names that clarify what the drug is. While there are millions of compounds, most doctors use only about thirty drugs. It is simply impossible for doctors, or anybody else for that matter, to be familiar with or even remember many drugs. The pharmaceutical companies label drugs with legal hold harmless statements that leave the patient or the doctor responsible for misuse.

Lawyers use Latin legal phrases such as *quid pro quo* instead of "a favor for a favor," *ad quod damnum* instead of "according to the harm," and *pro bono* for "free." I vividly recall my feeling of helplessness at several meetings listening to attorneys banter around legal terms while leaving the rest of us in the dark, not knowing what they were talking about and being afraid to ask questions. I needed a copy of *Black's Law Dictionary. Knowledge is power.* At times, it can and will be used against you.

So each discipline has its mode of operation. If you want to participate, you have to learn the jargon. For many years, it was virtually impossible for the average person to find reliable information relating professional jargon to easily understandable explanations. The Internet has changed all of that. Now we just need a few seconds to hit a key to find the meaning and explanation of any word using such tools as the *MSN Encarta Premium Dictionary* and *Wikipedia Free Encyclopedia.* You can even keep up with TV journalists by checking the Internet words of the day.

Now even average people like you and me can quickly find the meaning, or meanings, of any word. Such information is available to anyone, anyplace in the world. Try keeping an up-to-date list of new words. Periodically review the list. Learning is not only a lifelong necessity, but one of the great pleasures in life.

So, you can easily look up and find the proper definition of words. But there is more to language than just words. Intellectuals use such tools as the allegory and the metaphor. Such words may frighten those who don't understand their meaning. The meanings are simple. An *allegory* is a symbolic story that represents other things and expresses a deeper spiritual, moral, or political meaning. A *metaphor* is a symbol that represents something else. Some things represented are often understood only by people of a certain background or culture—someone educated to recognize the comparison or deeper meaning. It's like talking in code. To know what is being talked about, you must know the code.

And don't be confused by those who talk over you. Don't let others beat you down with spin. Keep trying to understand. Look at the details and try to figure it out. As Alfred Montapert put it, "The first lesson in the art of living is to *distinguish the important from the unimportant.*"

6 – EDUCATION

Reading, writing, and arithmetic—that's all there is. Those are the basics of formal academia. Master those three disciplines, and you are qualified to be considered an educated person.

Education sounds simple. By means of the spoken and printed word, we can benefit from the thoughts of those who have preceded us. We can profit from another's experience, though they lived in a different age and culture. Now, in the information age of the computer, education should be even easier.

Education sounds simple enough—just study hard and let it happen. But for many of us, that's not enough. While some of us excel academically beyond expectations, too many of us fail to perform up to our ability. Most people fail to achieve their best in school not because they don't try hard enough, but because they don't know how to study.

I attended a small-town school where grades one through twelve were all in the same building. I wasn't very diligent at studying in either grade school or high school. I tended to let my natural intellect take me as far as it could. It took me far enough to get into a state university. In college, however, I was shocked to find how poorly prepared I was to compete with kids from larger schools. For my first two years in college, I worked very hard, but I didn't get very good grades. I was afraid of failing. Then, with the help of a kind mentor, I learned how to study.

Successful learning depends on a multitude of things: natural intellect, past training, the effectiveness of the teacher, how tired you may be, how much other stress there is in your life, peer influence, the study group you are in or are not in, and the availability of tutors, among other things.

In my entire life, I had only four really good teachers, one in grade school, one in high school, and two in college. They taught me to enjoy learning and how to have confidence in myself. They all knew their subjects, they all had the ability to pass it on in a format I could understand, and they all projected an interest in me. I was also fortunate enough in my sophomore year of college to find a mentor. We studied separately but we studied in the same place, a quiet dormitory lounge. There it was easy to communicate when we needed to. He was brilliant, but he brought our discussions down to my level and tried to pull me to his. He did, and I graduated with a degree in civil engineering. I was able to do that only because I learned how to study and because I had mastered the basics of reading, writing, and arithmetic.

Reading is the process of identifying and understanding the characters and words in written or printed material. *Writing* is the activity of creating written works. Reading and writing pertain to all languages—English, French, German, or any of the thousands of distinct languages of the world. Reading comes easiest for the very young. Writing, of course, must await the development of proper motor skills; but the prime years to learn languages, and to learn to read, are ages two to about thirteen. At those ages, the brain readily accepts and remembers words, usually by association. As we mature, the brain begins to fill up with facts and learns more slowly and laboriously. The old practice of memorization is being replaced with association. Modern language instruction is by the interactive video computer, which encourages the reader to learn by doing. It automatically prompts and electronically pronounces words accurately. The goal, however, is the same as always—to think in the language you are trying to learn.

Unfortunately, for people like me, foreign language is difficult, if not impossible, to learn from a book or in the classroom. Some of our brains are just not geared to remember foreign words. People like me need logic, like in arithmetic.

Arithmetic is adding, subtracting, multiplying, and dividing. That's all there is. Those are the basics. With those four disciplines, you can perform any and all of mathematics, although often quite laboriously. To make it less laborious, we need advanced education.

Advanced education is education that teaches specialty concepts, shortcuts, and advanced concepts and details. Advanced education matures your thinking and provides you with specialty knowledge not necessarily needed or used by others. Subjects such as organic chemistry, sociology, philosophy, and calculus are examples of advanced education. *Professional education* is education that prepares you with the skills necessary to get and keep a job. English composition, structural analysis, and electrical design are examples of professional education. Subjects such as these are what you have prepared for your entire student life. These are truly meaningful and valuable subjects that employers seek and need. Professional education is what will put food on the table. *Continuing education* is lifelong learning. Learning never stops. Things change, and our knowledge must change with time. If we don't keep up, technology will bury us. We must stay current in professional matters, or we will find ourselves out of work and unable to provide for our families. This is true of any profession, but particularly pertains to technicians. *As technology changes, so must we.* We can never sit back and rest on our laurels. But we should always have in our head the basic skills needed if technology fails.

I know a little something about continuing education. In college, I worked long hours and studied hard to master the fundamentals and principles of engineering. The basic principles are still valid; they never change. But codes and computers soon made obsolete all of the specific professional procedures I had sacrificed so much to learn. It was a rude awaking to discover that I needed to spend more time and money to keep myself up-to-date enough to perform my job.

The most valuable continuing education is that which quickly, accurately, and economically gives you valuable current information. This may be found in books, computer software programs, college lectures, and convention programs, or on the Internet. You must be careful, however, to carefully evaluate the value of any continuing education course to *avoid an unnecessary waste of time and money.*

Sometimes education includes things that seem a waste of time. Early in my engineering career, I worked as a bridge design engineer. I learned the design codes and did my job. Then, after several years, we had no more bridge work. So I worked in a related field, water and wastewater treatment plant design. I knew very little about that field and basically had to teach myself, with a lot of vicious prodding by my superior. I worked in that field for many years; and just about the time I really knew what I was doing, that work ran out too. By that time, there was more bridge work, so I went back to again try my hand at bridge design. Upon returning to the bridge design field, I discovered the codes had changed radically and there were all new computer programs. If the code changes and computers weren't enough, the Department of Transportation decided to change from the English system of measurement to the metric. With much hardship, we turned out bridge plans in metric rather than English. The first thing the contractor did was to convert all dimensions back into English. It was a waste of time, but we got paid.

The school of hard knocks. Regardless of our schooling, we all have our share of hard knocks. The school of hard knocks may sometimes include embarrassment, regret, defeat, and failure. Some say it is in these moments that we learn the most. Sometimes that is true, but most often it is not.

I have perceived that good comes in bad times only if you are truly gaining experience and knowledge that will benefit you or your loved ones in the future. That happened to me in my professional career. I have worked for several rough bosses. They yelled at me, preached to me, and then took credit for my work. But I took it, and so did my family. Although the embarrassment and ridicule was almost unbearable, I took it because they had knowledge and they were passing it on. Then, in later years when they were long gone, I used the knowledge they had passed on to me and tried to pass a little of it on to any others who seemed interested.

I have also perceived that absolutely no good comes from bad times if you cannot successfully use what you have learned. Failure may occur for many reasons; some we can control, some we cannot. You may fail because of your lack of training, the lack of sufficient natural talent, the timing of your endeavor, the people you come in contact with, the lack of sufficient funds, the skill of your competition, or a hundred other reasons. When in such bad times you are locked into a situation from which it is impossible to extract yourself, you must find solace in the fact that you have sacrificed for others. You have failed so that others might win. You are a child of God in the game of life. God gave you the gift of decision making, the freedom to choose. You made your decisions. You lost. Don't forget, *there can't be a winner without a loser*. You lose for others; likewise, others lose for you. Your time to win will come.

Certain of us learn faster than others. Learning is a function of natural intellect. *Intellect*, also called intelligence, is the ability to think, reason, and understand. It is not the same as being smart; being *smart* is the ability to adapt to one's environment. It is not the same as being *clever*; being clever is the ability to creatively adapt. *Intelligence* includes the traits of knowledge and wisdom. Intellect is not merely book learning. Intellect is the ability to catch on, to make sense of things, to remember, and to figure out what to do. Intellect is the ability to apply knowledge in order to perform better in a particular environment.

IQ, or intelligence quotient, is a measure of intelligence as determined by aptitude testing on different aspects of intellectual functioning. IQ may vary from 50 to 150, with 100 being the average. IQ is a result mainly of genetic makeup, although environment, mental activity, and health are other contributing factors.

Quality education depends on many things we cannot control—such as who has the best teachers, the best mentors, the best fellow students; natural intellect and competition; and, of course, the teaching material used. Much of what we learn in school may soon be forgotten. That's okay if through it all, we have learned how to learn. It's not only the destination that matters; it's the journey. We must continue to learn through our entire lives.

Let's just be sure our educational efforts will not be in vain. Sometimes we can study too much on one subject. Don't lose sight of the forest for the trees. Avoid unnecessary confusion. Be aware of the difference between theory and reality. Recognize when so-called high tech is simply another name for job security. And when progress slows to the point that you have doubts, you may have reached the *point of diminishing returns*. If you have, just drop it and go to another subject, such as painting or weaving. Or maybe for a while you want to become an expert on soap operas, join a yoga club, or write a book. Just try to be sure what you are doing is worthwhile. That is when you can get the greatest joy from learning.

Throughout life we find things that make indelible impressions on us, either at school through our teachers or mentors, or through experience. Some of these impressions are good, and some are bad. The greatest injustice that can be done to anyone is to have a bad teacher. Students fear teachers because teachers rate them. It seems only right for students to rate teachers, such as is common in adult education. Teacher ratings should start in the first grade and continue through high school and college. We all deserve the best teachers available to prepare us to live in this sophisticated world. None of us can predict the future. All of us have to make the best of what we have. Sometimes you just have to *play the hand you're dealt*.

And don't confuse education with career success. History is often a product of economics, rather than ideas and intentions.

A lawyer once told me that when he graduated from high school, he knew everything; when he graduated from college, he knew something; but when he graduated from law school, he knew nothing. Unfortunately that is too often true. Sometimes *we learn more than the employment market will bear*. My father was a graduate electrical engineer. He graduated first in his class. He graduated in 1931. It was the depression. He never found a job. My grandfather had a farm, so my father became a chicken farmer and opened a hatchery. He never ever worked as an electrical engineer. He never ever had a job. He worked where there was a demand for him. He was an entrepreneur.

Life is short. Don't spend too much time learning unmarketable skills. Don't amass enormous college education debts to acquire unmarketable skills. *Put your time and money where it will do some good.* Study what you need to get a good and secure job. Study to learn what you need to know. Study to build character. Study for enjoyment. Education should be valuable, mentally stimulating, and enjoyable. Educating is easy, if you know the basics— reading, writing, and arithmetic.

7 – WORK

A lot of people do a lot of things they don't like for money.

Work is paid employment at a job or unpaid employment at home or at school. *In a perfect world, your vocation would also be your avocation.* But in this imperfect world, most of us have to work rather than play to make a living. Some of us work for others. Some are self-employed. Some work in our schools, colleges, and universities. Some of us are students, those who work to increase their ability to garnish a paying job of their own liking.

We spend at least one third of our lives working. We ought to enjoy it. Some of us do; some of us don't. Many of us view work as paid employment with specific duties. We leave our home and go to work for somebody else in exchange for money. Those who do usually do what they are told. If they do a good job in the eyes of their employer, they are given regular pay increases and, in some cases, increased responsibility.

The selection of a career path is one of the most important decisions we make in life. It affects our financial welfare, our general happiness, and our entire lifestyle. Unfortunately, when selecting a career path, we sometimes cannot recognize or properly analyze the ramifications of these three effects—financial welfare, lifestyle, and general happiness. Some of us are lucky enough to know exactly what we want to do in life. We prepare ourselves with the necessary education and experience to do what we think we want to do.

We can be an employee, or we can be an employer (boss). Most times things work out for the best. But sometimes they don't.

Employment is a contract between two parties, the master-slave relationship, except that slaves don't get paid, and employees do. Employees have the freedom to leave their employment, except when *"Baby needs a new pair of shoes."* The master is the boss; the boss cannot leave, and he directs and calls the shots. The employee does the work. Sometimes, as in the case of labor unions, there is a formal contract between employer and employee specifying the rights and duties of each. Most often, however, there is no formal contract. If you don't like that, you can quit. It is customary to give your employer two weeks notice, but you are not always required to do so. It's a free country. Being able to quit and walk away is an inherent right of the employee. But when we do, we have to be willing to take another job someplace else. We may not like it. We may have to take less pay, sometimes a lot less pay. But to survive, we have to work, have someone else provide financial support, or draw unemployment.

There are lots of advantages to employment, such as security, routine, and regular paydays. Most employees find happiness in getting into and losing themselves in the job. Employees tend to be happier than employers. When the day is over, employees go home and forget about it. I was always an employee, never an employer. I was fortunate to have thoughtful bosses who screened me from the insecurities and corruption of marketing and from the hassles of office politics. But there were times of concern.

Once, during a mild recession, I was worried that I might be laid off by my employer. My father-in-law told me, *"Do what the bosses want, and you'll be all right."* That turned out to be good advice.

Sometimes good advice is hard to recognize when we are employed. Sometimes some of us find ourselves in mean employments, employments that ask us to violate our basic moral principles. Terminate mean employments when possible. Plato said, *"Mean employments are a reproach,* because the individual is unable to control the creatures within him but has to court them, and his great study is how to flatter them." Terminate mean employments.

Employment should be a pleasant experience that brings not only financial rewards but pride, satisfaction, and personal progress. That also applies to employers. The employer is commonly thought of as management. But really, in large companies and in government, managers are just employees; managers just get paid more, work longer hours, and worry a lot.

For those of you who think you want to be managers for a major company, remember the stress, the long hours, the competition, the time involvement, and the natural intellect required. Large companies like GE and IBM look for high achievers and rate them on: 1) external factors, 2) clear thinking, 3) imagination, 4) inclusiveness, and 5) expertise. If you go this route, try to find a company that offers management training.

The real break comes with ownership. Ownership carries the assumption that the owner is all powerful, but nothing is further from the truth. Owners are responsible to their employees, as well as their clients. Owners often work twelve hours a day, six days a week. They also are totally responsible for business development, finance, and policy decisions. I learned from watching my father that ownership carries its own burdens, as well as the pleasure of being your own boss.

Then there are *entrepreneurs*, those who *possess and find new business ventures*. Potential rewards are great, but so are the risks. Successful entrepreneurship depends on a number of factors, such as timing, preparation, business plans, financing, environment, and luck. The entrepreneur assumes accountability for the risks and outcome of his venture. Entrepreneurs cannot merely walk away. The entrepreneur must first sell out or close up shop. But when successful, the entrepreneur can make lots of money and is his own boss. Even so, in this changing world, the entrepreneur must always be considering starting a new business or modifying an old one.

Whether you are an employee or an employer, there are lots of rewards from work other than financial. For some of us, there is pride of accomplishment. For others, there is satisfaction of service. For me, it was honor—although I rarely received it. During my working career, I became frustrated by the lack of honor and recognition. Others noticed my disappointment.

At one time, I was project engineer for design and construction of a new river water treatment plant to provide potable water to a large town. I had followed the job from the study stages through design and construction. During the shop drawing stage, a drawing came across my desk for approval of the bronze dedication plaque to be placed in the lobby of the treatment plant. The drawing listed the consulting engineer, the contractor, the mayor, the town council members, my boss, who was the engineer of record, and his boss, who was township engineer and principal of the design firm. At one time, the consulting architect was also to be listed, but his name was deleted because it was our job, not his, even though his ideas were the principal reason the job looked so good. I felt bad the architect's name had been deleted but was pleased to see listed at the bottom of the plaque my name and the title Project Engineer. I knew I should delete my name, but this was just the honor I thought I was looking for. So I decided to honor myself and approved the plaque layout with my name at the bottom. I did what my college president once advised, "*You have to do it yourself.*"

There are those who receive honor and those who honor. Those who are honored enjoy the benefits of recognition. Those who honor enjoy the benefits of power.

I wanted honor. Nobody else noticed or even cared, especially my wife. My wife never cared if I was the president or the janitor, but she expected me to bring home a paycheck and to be home every night at 5:15 for dinner and to spend time with the family. I couldn't always do that. Sometimes I had to work late. And when I came home, I needed to *debrief*. I needed to *let go of the stress*. Sometimes to let go of the stress, I drank.

It started with one drink, then two, then three or four drinks. Like the old saying about drinking goes, "*One is for ladies, two is for gentlemen, three is for pigs, and four is for jackasses.*" From personal experience, I have observed that men should *never drink more than two drinks once a week*, or maybe three on appropriate occasions. But never, ever have more than four drinks once a week. If you do, you will burn out your pancreas, your kidneys, and your liver. And *never, ever drink and drive.* The risks of liability are too high. If you have to drink to relax, you are in the wrong job. Find out what job you are good at, learn how much work stress you can comfortably handle without disrupting your family life, and then see what jobs like that are available. And *don't smoke.* I was tethered to a job for several decades because I was allowed to smoke. Smoking severely limits potential jobs available to you.

There is work, there is the business of work, and there is the politics of work. Most of us are good at at least one of these. Few of us are good at all three. Speaking for myself, I was good at work. I was a good worker. I was a terrible businessman. And I hated the politics of work. But I always had a job. I always had a job because I was willing to go where the work was (usually just around the corner). I did what I was told. After several mishaps, I learned to be professional. Remember, work is work. Don't joke around. Don't fool around. Just work. And *always be professional.* Don't be grumpy. Don't complain. Continually *update yourself* in new technologies applicable to your line of work. *Be nice to people.* And *always have your résumé ready.*

8 – FATE

Someone once joked, *"Fate is what happens while you're planning."*

There is a bit more to it than that, of course. There is fate, and there is destiny. Fate and destiny are often referred to interchangeably. Both refer to the outcome determined by outside events, but there is a difference. *Fate* refers to somebody's future as predetermined and inevitable by a series of events in which they do not participate. *Destiny*, on the other hand, refers to the outcome achieved by the person willfully participating.

If, for example, you undertake a major endeavor and give it all the energies and finances and time that you have, your success or failure is destiny. If, on the other hand, good or bad things happen that are beyond your control, your success or failure is fate. *Destiny implies choice. Fate implies no choice.*

Fate was more perfectly defined in a serious note by a very funny lady.

> *I wanted a perfect ending. Now I've learned, the hard way, that some poems don't rhyme, and some stories don't have a clear beginning, middle, and end. Life is about not knowing, having to change, taking the moment and making the best of it, without knowing what's going to happen next.*
>
> Gilda Radner

9 – POWER

The word *power* is one of those multiplicity-of-meanings words that tends to confuse until enough background is given to know which meaning applies. In this chapter, *power* refers to sociological power, or power in society. Sociological power means political, financial, or social power to control and influence other people and their actions. It also pertains to persuasiveness and skill.

Sociological *power is the ability to bring about significant change in people's lives*, our own or others'. It may exist in several forms: ability, knowledge, financial, force, delegated authority, sex, attractiveness, and rank, to name a few. Power may be exercised in several forms: decision making, agenda setting, influence, authority, coerciveness, persuasion, and direct force. The basis of power includes: formal authority, charisma, and expertise. Each of these may be classified as informational, rewarding, or coercive power. Informational is having information not attributable to your own expertise. Rewarding means your ability to offer rewards. Coerciveness refers to the ability to use force or threats.

The greatest power results from well-developed natural ability. Ability not only results in power, but it also attracts recognition, admiration, and honor. The able person is a true artist, somebody who does something skillfully and creatively. Ability is usually developed from natural talents. Exceptional ability may be developed from natural talent. Basic talent is in the genes, but the development of exceptional ability still takes work. It's great to be gifted with natural talent.

Then there are the rest of us. We must seek power on others' terms. We may be appointed, or we may win competitions—nature's way of selecting the most qualified. We may be well-liked by others. Or we may just be lucky. But most often, we have to acquire power ourselves. We have to be willing to pay the price. We have to be willing to work harder and longer than others. We have to make sacrifices.

Do you think you want power? For most of my life, I did—not because I wanted to control others, but because I wanted to control my own life and because I thought it would bring me honor and happiness. After many years, I concluded that, except for natural talent and developed ability, power brings resentment by many of those over whom you wield it. It will bring increased recognition and responsibility, if that is what you want. And while in some cases it may bring financial rewards, the honor and happiness accompanying those financial rewards only come after the increased responsibilities disappear.

Power should not be confused with honor. Power means control. Honor means respect and admiration. Power may include honor, or it may not. Power is all important, more important than being right; no matter how smart you are or how much you know, power is all important. Machiavelli recognized the importance of power when he wrote, *"An unarmed prophet will have his career end in disaster."*

Machiavelli was a pragmatic, no-nonsense, take-no-prisoners brutal political philosopher. He left us some important advice for those in power, such as: *"Whoever is responsible for another becoming powerful ruins himself. A prince should delegate to others the enactment of unpopular measures and keep in his own hands the means of winning favors. And a prince should strive to demonstrate in his actions grandeur, courage, sobriety, and strength; at the same time, he should avoid doing anything that will make him hated and despised."*

If you are a political person, always take a side in political actions. If you want power, don't stand on the sidelines of political campaigns. Machiavelli's advice was, "If you do not declare yourself, you will always be at the mercy of the conqueror. The conqueror does not want doubtful friends, while the loser repudiates you because you were unwilling to throw your lot with him. When you boldly declare your support for one side and that side conquers, he is under obligation to you. If your ally is defeated, he will shelter you and will help you while he can; and you will become associates whose joint forces may well change for the better."

Recognize and respect political power. If you want political power, go seek it, if you are willing to pay the price. But remember the old saying: *"Be careful what you ask for, because you just might get it."*

I once had a brilliant boss who desired power. He got it. I thought he was a good leader because he met his responsibilities to turn out a good job for the client. But other people working for him and in partnership with him did not. He was arrogant and bossy, and displayed no compassion or empathy. He was asked to leave.

I sought power on several occasions. On every occasion, I regretted it. I regretted it because I get no thrill from power. I get thrill from honor.

If you don't want political power, sit back and smell the roses. Let somebody else change your life. Use what power is naturally yours. Exercise it when appropriate, and for only the right reasons.

10 – CONFLICT

Conflict is a clash between opposing interests, actions, and values to determine outcome—who wins and who loses, who gets what they want and who doesn't, what values govern and what values are forsaken. Conflict is a part of life. Some of us love it; some of us hate it.

Conflict begins at a young age. It begins in school. It begins on the playground. It begins on the ball field. It begins in the classroom and with report cards. It begins in the hallways and at the school dances. It's called competition, nature's way of selecting the best, nature's way of selecting the smartest, the most athletic, and the best looking. It is through conflict that we choose our professions, our careers, our friends, and our mates. Conflict may be external between individuals or internal within one's self. We may compete with others for needs, status, goals, and glory. We may compete within ourselves to choose our most precious values.

It is this *clash* that produces emotion—the intertwined behavioral, physiological, and cognitive consequences of conflict. Conflict involves emotion because something triggers it, usually some type of action by another party. The conflict is with the parties and how they seek to resolve it. There are five ways to resolve conflict: accommodation, avoidance, collaboration, compromise, and competition.

You may *accommodate* the other party by surrendering to his demands. This is the lose-win solution. You lose; they win. This is usually reserved for minor conflicts. I recall one time at the grocery store: after I had taken my number at the deli counter, I strolled away for a few minutes. When I returned, I noticed my number had come up on the display board so I held up my ticket and announced that I was here. Some obese lady standing next to me announced I was not present when my number came up so she should go next. The other customers waiting in line watched closely to see what I would do. In order to avoid argument and a scene, I let her go ahead of me. It was more valuable to me to let her win rather than continue the conflict. Accommodation is often the best and easiest way out of a minor conflict.

You can *avoid* the conflict. If you are not prepared to win, walk away. Compete only when you are comfortable competing. You can't win all the time. *Pick your battles.*

You can *collaborate* and work together to find mutually acceptable solutions. Collaboration is the only win-win solution. It is often used by people who constantly seek a more accurate and better way of doing things. But it often takes time to find a mutually beneficial solution, sometimes more time than you have. Collaboration takes time, trust, respect, and good communication.

You can *compromise*. You can find ground on which each party is partly satisfied. This is what politicians do. This is what they get paid for. Sometimes it works out to initially ask for more than you want and then settle for what you really want.

Or you can *compete*. You can aggressively seek to achieve your objectives at the expense of the other party. You can fight, hoping to win. But you must also be prepared to lose. On the juvenile level, there is nothing better than being first chair, if you have the talent, the preparation, and the time to handle it. Otherwise, you are better off not playing first chair and will be happier.

On the athletic field, things are different. Here the whole team wins or loses together. The chain is only as strong as its weakest link, so you don't want to be the weakest link. With athletics there is supposed to be something called good sportsmanship. Don't believe it. Only winners savor the glory of victory. Only the losers suffer defeat.

In military conflict, winning and losing is for keeps. Once the shooting starts, there is no compromise on the battlefield. It is kill or be killed. Soldiers are scared. When in doubt, soldiers kill. Soldiers are not humanitarians. Missionaries are humanitarians. Soldiers are trained to kill and, when necessary, to die. War is for keeps.

In adult life, conflict is also for keeps but is more forgiving. Losers can move away and start over. Winners are locked in.

All of this sounds straightforward and simple. But it is neither straightforward nor simple, because conflict evokes emotion, sometimes extreme and lasting emotion. Nobody wants to lose.

I always try to think rationally in a conflict. I always try to figure the odds and decide if it is worth the risk of conflict. I, like everybody else in the world, must and will protect my own interests, because nobody else will protect them for me; nobody else cares.

I have come to realize that more often than not, it is the rules of nature that determine the eventual outcome of a conflict. Winners will be those with the most talent, those with the most resources, those with the best judgment, those willing to devote productive time, and those willing to maintain steady pressure and perseverance even when threatened or faced with failure, those who never give up. The eventual winners are those who try always to improve their skills, expand their resources, and never quit. Those are the real winners.

Above all, be patient. As Plato said, "To *be patient* under suffering is best. Nothing is gained by impatience."

II – POLITICS

Politics involves conflict. Without conflict, there is no politics.

Politics refers to *conflict management* and *conflict resolution* in our lives, our governmental, professional, and private lives—dealing with others in government, at work, and at home. Politics has to do with who wins, who rules. In that regard, we most often think of professional politicians.

Professional politicians include anybody who is involved in public decision making. They include members of government, anybody whose main political motive is self-advancement, and schemers (people who manipulate relationships). Most often we think of politicians as members of a branch of government.

The state is the highest form of government. Government types vary according to political attributes. They include: autocracy or rule by one (monarchy, dictatorships); oligarchy or rule by minority; democracy or rule by majority; and anarchism or rule by no one. A republic is any form of government in which all or some portion of the people rule.

Political rule is supposed to aim primarily at the *highest good* of those who are ruled. Oligarchy is the rule of the rich; democracy is the rule of the poor. Aristotle believed that both miss the true object of the state, which is virtue. He taught that *workings in the way of virtue are what determine happiness.* Ideally, *the highest good is happiness.* Aristotle also taught that all citizens had political power and that a good citizen knows both how to rule and how to obey.

Plato, on the other hand, taught that all forms of government demonstrate one simple principle of justice—that which is in the interest of the stronger. Plato taught that any political system is essentially a set of arrangements by which some people dominate others.

Governmental politics, as opposed to civil service, is primarily concerned with power—the power to affect our own lives and the lives of others. Traditionally, the goal of political activity was to resolve conflict in a way that results in the highest greater good. In other words, do what is best for most of the people. This lofty goal results in some people winning and some losing. That's just the way it is.

In political campaigns, one person wins and one person loses. One person gains power to make decisions, and the other retires to obscurity. There is no win-win outcome in political campaigns. There is only a winning side and a losing side. The winning side is where people who can't get elected dogcatcher get appointed to influential and decision-making positions.

Some of us look down on the politics of civil government as a nasty business. Those who do may perceive that governmental politics repels the best people and attracts the worst. But it was not always that way.

Aristotle believed that citizens must actively participate in politics if they are to be happy and virtuous. Aristotle believed man is a political animal. He also believed that ethics and politics were closely linked, and that the role of politics is to provide an environment in which people can live fully ethical and happy lives. Aristotle taught that the aim of politics should be to develop virtue in its citizens to the greatest extent possible.

Plato, on the other hand, believed that only a few are suitable to rule, that only a few are gifted with the innate talent to govern. He also saw that justice is always in the interest of the stronger; the ruler always commands that which is in his own best interest. Right behavior is whatever those in power determine it to be. Plato taught that there were two types of just behavior: behavior of ordinary individuals and of those in political power. He also taught that rulers will find it necessary to disperse a mild dose of falsehood and deceit for the good of their subjects.

Then along came Machiavelli. Machiavelli taught that the end justifies the means. Machiavelli taught that for a prince to maintain his rule, he must be prepared to not be virtuous. He must destroy his enemies. But he must always be perceived as a person of compassion, a man of integrity, a man of good faith, and a kind and gentle man.

These different philosophies have been taught for hundreds of years and are still taught in colleges today.

So, what types of people are best suited for governmental politics? First of all, they must have great intellect. If they don't, intellect will be used against them, both by the opposition and by the media. Second, they must be totally immune to criticism. Criticism must flow off of them like the proverbial water off a duck's back. Third, they must be insensitive to others' feelings—they must be willing to hurt others. Fourth, they must have the ability to not lose track of the forest for the trees; they must be able to quickly identify what is important and to focus on that. Fifth, they must be faithful to their political party. Sixth, they must be willing to compromise. Seventh, they must be decisive. And last but most important, they must be eloquent speakers. They must be able to speak endlessly and say nothing. They are most often born bullshit artists and remain bullshit artists the whole of their lives. It also helps to be good-looking.

Would you make a good politician? Do you have any of the aforementioned attributes? You may have the talent to be a politician, but do you want the political life? Always remember that as a politician, half of the people love you but the other half hates you. You will always be a lightning rod for others to vent their anger. Remember, also, that power is not the same as honor and has absolutely nothing to do with happiness.

Workplace politics is similar in nature to governmental politics in that its goal is to acquire power and influence, but it differs in one major aspect—the loser is not banished; he merely cowers to the winner in exchange for a job. In politics of the workplace, there is often room for win-win outcomes. But ultimately, somebody has to win. If Joe wins, it may be because he has superior talents, has nurtured alliances, or has money. Most often, however, the winner in the workplace is a master of political strategy and tactics.

Strategy is how to put yourself in the right place at the right time. *Tactics* is what you do when you get there. You must understand both. You must recognize what they are and learn to deal with them.

Common *political strategies* include buying power, donating time, developing valuable career alliances by brownnosing the right people and destroying others, and compromise.

In politics, perception is truth. It usually doesn't matter what's right or wrong. Great masses of people worshipped Adolph Hitler. People undyingly supported John Kennedy, Richard Nixon, and Bill Clinton, regardless of their personal behavior or their policies. For some reason, many people just liked them. Others just hated them.

Political tactics used depend on the situation. Common tactics used in political campaigns include overstating or understating facts, issuing misleading information, overemphasizing the positive or the negative, innuendo, partial truths, and just outright lying. As far back as Plato, educators have taught that lying is best to keep great masses of people happy. When asked an embarrassing question, change the subject. Answer only the questions you want to answer. Answer only questions you are prepared to answer.

Political winners use a variety of methods to acquire and hold power. They take credit for other people's work. They use intimidation. They use their advantage of intellect or good looks to impress or defeat others. They strive to make others look good or look bad. They play on fears and divisions. They help others without increasing their strength. They crush the powerful.

All of this must seem overwhelming. What is the little guy supposed to do to overcome such tactics? Well, for starters, *pick your battles*. Meet on the playing field of your choice. And then be relentless and unapologetic. As sad as it is, that is what politicians must do. They must defeat the enemy, taking no prisoners.

Through all of this, you must ask yourself, "Is it worth it? Is this what I really want to do? Do I have the necessary intellect to compete? Do I have the instinct to kill? Am I comfortable lying?"

How can the rest of us deal with this? We must learn to recognize the bullshit artist for what he is. Do not let yourself be swayed by prejudiced journalists and so-called TV news commentators, many of whom are just entertainers. Do not be intimidated. Never be afraid to enter the fray on your terms, or to counter aggressive opposition. But do not, under any circumstances, destroy your integrity. Recognize and accept the outcome. And when it is over, forget it all.

Personal politics is the politics of dealing with family and friends. There is only one rule in personal politics—love your neighbor as yourself. Be kind. Be gentle. Be honest. Be understanding. Love makes all things right. All personal politics involves love.

12 – JUSTICE

Justice means *fairness in the way people are treated*. Fairness is wired into our brains. It is part of our natural makeup. Fairness satisfies a basic need for the proper ordering of things and persons in a society. But who, exactly, decide what fairness is?

Aristotle argued that a just person is one who follows the concept of *moral rightness based on ethics*. He argued that justice is the course of action that the moral aim of the state requires.

Plato, on the other hand, argued that justice is merely that which is in the interest of the stronger. The ruling power is responsible for determining what just behavior is. In different forms of government (democratic, aristocratic, tyrannical), there is the one simple principal justice—that which is in the *interest of the stronger*.

Aristotle and Plato agreed that justice must cover both the just person and the just state. There are two kinds of just behavior—that of ordinary individuals and that of those in political power.

As far back as the early Greek philosophers, and even further back, justice has been demanded in the form of giving people what they deserve, or retributive justice—why punish, who gets punished, and what punishment should they receive. Traditionally, justice has meant the repayment of debts. As society progressed, institutions were formed where people were interconnected, but they disagreed.

Now we deal with more sophisticated variations of justice, including restorative justice (helping the offender) and distributive justice (determining the proper allocation of things such as wealth and power). What is the proper ordering of things and persons in a society? What is the proper distribution of wealth and resources?

For most of us, justice simply means the repayment of a debt. People are due what they are owed for their time, for their labor, for their service, and for their loss due to others' neglect. Some may tend to think of justice as revenge for a loss due to others' neglect. But justice is not revenge. *Revenge* means the punishment of somebody in retaliation for harm done. Revenge has nothing to do with fairness. Justice has to do with fairness in the way we treat other people, but justice is not fairness.

Very little in this life is fair. Some of us are smarter than others. Some of us are better looking than others. Some of us are wealthier or in better health than others. No, justice has nothing to do with fairness. Justice has to do with fairness in the way people are treated. Each of us is responsible for our own morality and the moral standards we use in treating others. For most of us, the rule is simple, *"Do unto others as you would have them do unto you"* and demand the same.

For everything else, there are laws.

13 – LAW

During my lifetime, I have been in court seven times: once as a juvenile defendant before a magistrate for a minor traffic violation, once as a defendant before a family court judge for underage drinking, once as a juror in a murder trial, once before a municipal judge for a moving traffic violation, and three times as an expert witness. As a professional engineer, I testified as an expert witness in court for construction claims and professional malpractice. I must say that from those experiences, I gained an appreciation for the legal profession.

There are man-made laws for practically everything. Man-made laws are *enforceable rules* of conduct for society, and they are binding and enforceable by authority. Man-made law has, as its root, legislation passed by a legislature or similar body. Man-made laws and their resulting regulations are written down to tell you what you are allowed or not allowed to do. This system of rules shapes politics and economics and serves as social mediator in relations between people.

Laws are neatly filed to allow easy access to them—if, that is, you know where to look and how to interpret what you are looking at. Unfortunately, there is a lot to look at. Our laws are written by trained lawyers who protect their profession by overcomplicating the simple with confusing legal terms such as those listed in the thirteen-hundred-page *Black's Law Dictionary*.

It is well-known that the bulk of law work is data management—finding out and remembering what is going on. It used to be impossible for the average citizen to research federal and state laws unless they had good and lengthy access to a law library. Now, much is available on the Internet. Legal information formerly available only to the privileged is now available to all.

Legal basics are boring. But then, *good government is boring*. So read on; it's only three pages.

Constitutional law pertains to affairs of state. The US Constitution spells out in a few pages exactly what our basic rights are and how the federal government is organized into three branches: the legislative branch or the Congress (House and Senate) to enact laws, the administrative branch to enforce the laws, and the judicial branch to interpret the laws. State government is set up the same as federal government.

Statutes are laws enacted by the legislature. *Regulations* are rules issued by the executive branch in accordance with legal statutes. State regulations are normally bound together as the *administrative code*. Administrative codes are often made difficult by cross-reference, so that you need to search several publications to glean the information you are looking for.

Laws are so massive they are broken down into subcategories:

Criminal law—what to do with the bad guys.

Contract law—promises.

Tort law—civil wrongs.

Property law—possessions.

Equity and trusts—properties or money held and managed by another.

International law—relationships between sovereign nations.

There are, of course, specialty categories, such as law and society, law and commerce, and law and regulation—all of which are further broken down into specific specialties, such as intellectual property, tax law, and environmental law.

Unfortunately, there are thousands of federal and state laws and hundreds of thousands of federal and state regulations—and we are still passing more laws and issuing new regulations. Such a bureaucracy creates an overwhelming burden for the average person to understand what is going on, let alone know what laws and regulations there are. You may choose to research specific laws and regulations by yourself, but you will need a lawyer to impact the system.

Lawyers are officers of the court. As such, they play a most important role in the legal system. They are a part of the legal system but are paid directly by the client. Such an arrangement has created a myriad of conflicts requiring professional attention. This is called job security.

The *U.S. Declaration of Independence* of 1776 speaks of self-evident truths (natural laws of right and wrong), including that all men are created equal (nobody has superior rights over anybody else). It declares that the Creator has endowed each of us with unalienable (impossible to take away) rights, which include the right to life, liberty, and the pursuit of happiness (to live, to be free, and to purse happiness in any way we want so long as we do not infringe upon others' rights to do the same). Be sure to read the Declaration of Independence. It is a marvel of political prowess (great skill and ability); an insult and indictment of our former ruler, the king of England; and an insult to the "merciless Indian savages" of our then frontiers. The words of this great document called for, and justified, either rightly or wrongly, war.

The *U.S. Constitution* of 1789 was drafted as our country's ultimate law. It spells out how government is arranged (legislative, executive, and judicial branches). The Bill of Rights was added in 1791 to spell out what the government can and cannot do to interfere with our freedom to life, liberty, and the pursuit of happiness. Later amendments were added to abolish slavery and to give women the right to vote. At the presidential inauguration, the president of the United States swears to protect and defend the constitution.

Federal laws and regulations have been developed to specify federal taxes to finance the government, the military, infrastructure construction, and necessary measures to transfer wealth from the haves to the have-nots; as well as numerous measures to ensure we do not infringe upon another's rights to life, liberty, and the pursuit of happiness.

State statutes and regulations cover all other legal matters not covered under federal law, such as criminal law, contract law, tort law, property law, and equity and trusts. Each state is different, and each law reflects the moods of the times. For example, many state laws of 1860 specified different punishments for black people or mulattos than for white people. Today's laws protect the rights of all people, including homosexuals.

The bulk of our laws are state laws. State law greatly affects all of us—from the taxes we pay, to how we provide for the poor, to the rules by which we live. Federal laws guarantee us the freedoms to which state laws must conform. We may have, however, reached the point of diminishing returns in that many laws now seem to be written based on somebody's whim. Since it has been interpreted that the *government cannot do anything it is not authorized to do by law*, our elected officials pass many frivolous laws that, rather than protect our rights, actually take our rights away. In addition, the massive amount of statutes and regulations is so voluminous that the average citizen needs a lawyer to impact the system. The best most of us can do is to "Do unto others as you would have them do unto you"—if, that is, you are inclined to. If not, you better know the law, or you better have a good lawyer.

14 – ORDERS OF MAGNITUDE

You may be wondering why "orders of magnitude" have been included in this book.

INCREASING UNITS ORDER OF MAGNITUDE			
Number (Exponent)	Name	Metric Prefix	Metric Equivalent Per Single Unit
1 (10^0)	One	Meter	3'3"
1,000 (10^3)	Thousand	Kilo- K	5/8 mile
1,000,000 (10^6)	Million	Mega- M	620 miles
1,000,000,000 (10^9)	Billion	Giga- G	25 times around the earth
1,000,000,000,000 (10^{12})	Trillion	Tera- T	Seven times distance from earth to sun
1,000,000,000,000,000 (10^{15})	Million Billion	Peta- P	1/10 light-year
1,000,000,000,000,000,000 (10^{18})	Billion Billion	Exa- E	100 light-years

What do orders of magnitude have to do with anything? Well, a lot. Orders of magnitude should greatly influence our impressions, thoughts, and decisions.

Everybody knows the difference between one and ten. We all have ten fingers. So if we hold up one finger, it's easy to see the difference between one and ten. It is common to refer to measurements in terms of ten units, because we can then count them on two hands. Whether you use feet or meters, whether you use pounds or kilograms, the common increment is ten: 10, 100, 1,000, 10,000, 100,000, 1,000,000. If one finger represents one, then ten fingers represent ten. If one finger represents one hundred thousand, then ten fingers represent one million. It is also common to represent these exponentially: 10^1 (10×1), 10^2 ($10 \times 10 = 100$), 10^3 ($10 \times 10 \times 10 = 1,000$), and so on. And remember, any positive number raised to the zero power equals one.

So, what does one million dollars mean to you? Well, for most of us, it's a lot of money. But what about a billion? What about a trillion? For most of us, such magnitudes are incomprehensible.

In today's high-tech world, even the average person needs to understand and appreciate orders of magnitude, and to feel comfortable with them.

I like to think in terms of space and time. You can take one step and go about three feet in one second. You could take one hundred steps and go the length of a football field in a minute and a half. You can take one thousand steps and go about five-eighths of a mile in sixteen minutes. You can take one million steps and go 620 miles in twelve days (walking twenty-four hours per day). You can take one billion steps and go twenty-five times around the earth in thirty-three years.

Of course, if you travel those distances at the speed of light, you would arrive at each destination immediately, because time stops for a traveler traveling at the speed of light.

We can perform the same simple exercises by going the other way, to fractions. Hold up ten fingers and then close all but one. If all fingers represent one, then one finger represents one tenth. If ten fingers represent one tenth, then one finger represents one hundredth. Again, for units less than one, the common increment is ten: 1/10, 1/100, 1/1,000, 1/10,000, 1/100,000, 1/1,000,000. It is also common to represent these exponentially: 10^{-1} (1/10), 10^{-2} (1/100), and so on.

The term *macroscopic* refers to things we can see with the naked eye. That is about one micron, one fifth the diameter of a spider's web. *Microscopic* refers to things we can see only with a microscope. With an optical microscope, we can see down to about 0.2 microns (200 nanometers), or small enough to see typical bacteria removed by a surgical mask. Below that we need instruments that produce images of particles indicated rather than actually seeing the particles. Such instruments include the electron microscope, which uses electro bombardment to view particles as small as an atom.

DECREASING UNITS ORDER OF MAGNITUDE			
Number (Exponent)	**Name**	**Metric Prefix**	**Metric Equivalent Per Single Unit**
1 (10^0)	One	Meter	39 3/8″ 100 centimeters
1/1,000 (10^{-3})	Thousandth	Milli-	1/3 of 1/16 of an inch 1/10 centimeter
1/1,000,000 (10^{-6})	Millionth (Microns)	Micro- M	1/5 the width of a spider's web
1/1,000,000,000 (10^{-9})	Billionth	Nano- N	½ the diameter of a DNA helix
1/1,000,000,000,000 (10^{-12})	Trillionth	Pico- P	1/25 the width of a hydrogen atom
1/1,000,000,000,000,000 (10^{-15})	One Million Billionth	Femto- F	Size of a proton
1,000,000,000,000,000,000 (10^{-18})	One Billion Billionth	Atto- A	Size of an electron

15 – BODY, MIND, AND SOUL

Most of us rarely think about the body, mind, or soul—including me. For most of my life, I didn't even know the difference. All I knew was that the souls of good people go to heaven, while the souls of bad people go to hell. Heaven is eternal bliss in a city of gold streets. Hell is eternal suffering in a pit of fire. I learned from my parents to obey the Ten Commandments, be nice to people, and work hard—that advice works pretty well in both good times and bad. I learned from church that there are no good people, we are all sinners, and the only way we can go to heaven is to accept Jesus Christ as our savior—that also works pretty well in both good times and bad. I learned in school that we are all creatures of evolution; we evolved from an amoeba, and we aren't really much different from a monkey. For me, that has never worked, either in good times or bad.

We may look like monkeys. Our genes may be not much different from a monkey's, but we are not monkeys. We are not animals. We are intelligent human beings, a unique creation of God. Animals are of body and mind. Animals live only in the present. We live in the past, present, and future, and forever. We are of body, mind, and soul.

BODY

Like everything in the universe, we are made up of *atoms and molecules*, just like rocks, sand, and stones. But unlike rocks, sand, and stones, we are living organisms. The atoms and molecules in our body make up individual *living cells*. These cells form *tissue* (groups of similar cells), some of which form *organs* (several different types of tissue arranged to perform several functions). The human body is composed of over 65 percent water, about 18 percent carbon, and various amounts of other minor but critical elements.

Cells are the basic unit of living things. These smallest independently functioning units consist of one or more nuclei surrounded by cytoplasm (the gelatinous fluid that fills much of the volume of cells), all enclosed by a permeable membrane. Each cell is somewhat self-contained and self-maintained. It takes in nutrients, converts nutrients to energy, carries out various functions, and reproduces as necessary. The human body contains about 100 trillion cells.

There are about twenty different types of cells in the human body. Some cells are stationary; some cells move around. Cells vary in size from 1/2,500 of an inch for blood cells to thin filaments a few inches long in the central nervous system. Inside the cells are organelle, "little organs," such as the nucleus (houses chromosomes and organized structures of protein and DNA), ribosomes (which produce proteins), and mitochondria (energy generators), all of which permit the cell to flourish and reproduce. Cells normally reproduce and die away regularly. Blood cells reproduce and die away about every four months. Skin cells reproduce and die away about every thirty-five days. *Cell reproduction at a more rapid, uncontrolled rate is called cancer.*

Each individual cell contains genetic instructions for function and reproduction. These instructions are contained in a molecule called *DNA*. The DNA segments that carry genetic information are called *genes*. DNA and genes provide development and operating instructions to the body structure.

The body structure is merely a mass of atoms and molecules formed into bones, muscles, and fat. Alone, the body structure is just that, a useless mass of form. This mass is given function by, and only by, the central nervous system, an internetwork of sensors and activators called neurons. These sensors and activators send and receive instructions to and from the brain.

The brain is what we are—a bunch of brain cells. This bunch of brain cells performs two basic functions. First is to stimulate and control muscles and body parts through the spinal cord. (Every muscle in the body is controlled by the brain through the central and peripheral nervous systems.) Second, it is the site of reason and intelligence.

The brain is composed of two types of *brain cells*: *neurons*, which generate action potentials, and *glia*, which forms the glue that forms a support system for the neurons. *Neurons* are electrically active brain cells that process information. Brain cells of the central nervous system are commonly called *nerve cells*. For all practical purposes, brain cells and nerve cells have the same basic structure. They are all basically neurons.

Neurons are about one fifth the diameter of the human hair and vary in length from very short to up to a meter long. The cell body contains the nucleus, mitochondria, and other organelle, and is shaped as a long tubular body called an *axon*. There are chemical *receptors* (dendrites) at one end and chemical *transmitters* (synaptic knobs) at the other. The cell acts like a receiver, transmission line, and transmitter, all in one.

The neuron consists of a nucleus (a membrane-encased mass containing *DNA* (the chromosomes and other genetic information necessary to control cell growth and reproduction), dendrites (multiple short strings that receive signals from other neurons), and axons (single long, slender projections of the nerve cell, or axon, which transmit on or off signals to other neurons).

There are over 100 billion neurons in the human brain. Each neuron is linked to at least a thousand and as many as ten thousand other neurons. The brain is the physical mechanism in which the mind operates and the soul manifests itself in human activity.

MIND

Mind is the brain at work. Mind refers to intellect and consciousness. It is the center of thought and reason, the center of cognition or the processing of information.

Nerve cells and brain cells are electrochemical devices. A signal is received at one end when *ions* (atoms or molecules that are positively or negatively charged) are sensed by the *dendrites*. These ions energize the cell with voltage (action potential) that, when large enough (about 70 millivolts), causes an *electric charge* to move down the *axon* to the *synapse*. At the synaptic end, the charge ionizes certain elements that pass through the permeable membrane to ionize other nerve cells. The chemicals released are called *neurotransmitters*. The brain and the entire central nervous system operate as an electrochemical device.

Much of what we know about the brain today has been developed from research data collected as brain waves. We know, in a general way, what areas of the brain are used for what. Much of the mind is used for sight—that blessed miracle from God that allows us to interact with the world. Much of the mind controls our bodily movements and functions. Then there is what we call mental faculties—including consciousness, thought, memory, and imagination.

Axons, once activated, search for other cells to connect with. They look for cells that put out welcome mats and bypass cells without welcome mats or that have put out no-trespassing signs. Welcome signs need to be created and nourished. Once finding a welcome mat, these dendrites connect. Cell connections need to be exercised. *Connections* that are *not strengthened by stimulations die off.* In other words, the brain needs to learn how to make itself work. This is especially true in children.

Research suggests that the number of brain cell connections made may be increased by as much as 25 percent when properly nurtured. Evidence indicates the more brain cells you have connected, the smarter you are. Research also indicates that through proper exercise, even basic IQ can be somewhat increased.

IQ (intelligence quotient) is a measure of intelligence (also called intellect). IQ is measured by standardized tests, which rate one's IQ against others through a bell curve (average people in the middle, few at each end). IQ varies from 50 to 150, with the average intelligence being 100. IQ is a measure of one's innate ability to think and learn, to learn and recall facts and skills, and to apply them. It is not a measure of one's ability to succeed or to be happy.

The brain is the physical structure that produces electromagnetic signals to collect, store, and use information. It produces *thought*—the process by which we model the world and deal with it according to our desired goals, plans, and ends. It produces *memory*—the ability to store, retain, and recall information. Things are stored in memory not as pictures, but as discrete units of information that, when patched together, produce a picture. It allows for *imagination*—an innate ability to invent imagined personal interactions derived from an imagined world. It produces *consciousness*—the ability to perceive the relationship between oneself and the real world.

SOUL

The soul is the nonphysical aspects of a person—your consciousness, *your private thoughts, your feelings, your passions, your spirit.*

Since nothing is really known about the soul, it may have different meanings to each of us. For me, the soul is that sacred aura surrounding each of us that permits us to communicate with ourselves, with others afar, and with God.

Many people, including myself, believe the soul is eternal. It survives after death to be subject to happiness or misery in a life to come. A very religious man once squeezed the skin on my arm and said, "Someday, all of this will turn to dust." And it does. Only the soul can live forever.

It is the soul that exhibits emotions. Even a baby smiles when he feels love. Even a baby cries when he feels rejected. The soul thrives on love. The soul is damaged by rejection.

So, what is the soul? We don't know exactly, but we know it is something powerful. It is the moral and emotional part of man's nature, the seat of feeling, as distinguished from intellect, the whole person designed in the image of God. Some do not believe in the soul; some believe it is solely a product of the brain, a natural part of our intellect, of our rational and irrational being. Others believe in the soul as a spirit separate from our physical being, and believe that the brain is merely the mechanism by which the soul manifests itself and that the brain is the mechanism that influences the soul. What we do know is that the soul, whatever it is, needs to be nurtured.

It is when we nurture the soul with reverence that we find true success and happiness. Reverence means engaging in a contact of life that goes deeper than the shell of form and mass. Reverence is an attitude of honoring life. Reverence is a holy perception that allows us to see the significance of each living creature. When you are fully reverent, you cannot harm life. Reverence automatically brings forth patience. Reverence does not allow us to perceive ourselves as more or less superior or more important than any other person. Reverence is not an emotion, but reverence affects emotions. And it is emotion that reflects our intentions. It is important to make an effort to move toward the soul.

Much research has been undertaken and is still in progress investigating the belief that the soul is a nonphysical entity. Entire industries have been developed and flourish in great part due to the concept of soul; they include religion and elements of psychology and philosophy.

Other research has been conducted to evaluate whether or not the soul is in part a physical entity. Somebody even weighed humans before and after death and reported the weight of the soul is 21 grams. Few believe that, of course, but the number is interesting. If 21 grams of mass were converted to energy, that would equal the energy of over 100 kilotons of TNT, or six Hiroshima bombs.

Some heavy thinkers imagine there is a black hole within each of us to where our soul retreats upon death and travels to another universe at speeds faster than the speed of light. Under this assumption, our soul could arrive anyplace in the universe immediately. Even if the data held tight in the soul traveled only at the speed of light, the soul could arrive anywhere immediately because time stops at the speed of light. The transfer of data through space at the speed of light is a miracle. But to see and experience anything, the soul must stop someplace.

As I get older, this world seems smaller and smaller. I have traveled enough to know how small and limited this earth really is. I realize, too, the enormous size of the universe. For me, the entire universe is just waiting to be seen and experienced.

It would take only one coded DNA received in the right place to allow each of us to be born anew. It would take only a few brain waves traveling at the speed of light to determine our spiritual destiny. Depending on the condition of the soul at the time of death, we might land in heaven or in hell. A baby's soul is pure. So it is, to some extent, with those who lead the kind of life that nurtures the soul.

I am not trying to preach to you. I am not trying to direct your mind and thoughts. I am merely saying, "Yes, I believe there is a soul." None of us knows for sure, but many of us have faith. It's called religion.

16 – RELIGION

Religion pertains to people's beliefs, opinions, and worship of a deity or *God.* It also pertains to the divine or godlike involvement in the world and the universe.

Religion pertains to the spiritual world and universe, *spiritual* meaning *relating to the soul,* in contrast to material things.

There are many formal and informal religions in the world. Most people join a formal religious organization and try to lead a life that follows its teachings. Religion can be the thread that binds us together or the force that tears us apart. And there are a lot of us for those purposes. There are about 7 billion people in the world—7,000,000,000 = 7×10^9. That is an astounding number.

Approximate 2010 WORLD POPULATION DISTRIBUTION			
Location	Percentage	Population	
Asia	60.0%	4,200,000,000	4.2 billion
Africa	14.3%	1,000,000,000	1 billion
Europe	10.7%	750,000,000	0.75 billion
South America and Caribbean	7.9%	550,000,000	0.55 billion
United States	4.3%	300,000,000	0.3 billion
North America (except U.S.)	2.1%	150,000,000	0.15 billion
Oceania	0.7%	50,000,000	0.05 billion
TOTAL	100%	7,000,000,000	7 billion
Populations projected from 2009 Wikipedia statistics			

About 88 percent of these people follow a formal religion.

Approximate 2010 RELIGIOUS POPULATION DISTRIBUTION				
Religion	Percentage	Population		Primary Locations
Christianity	30.00%	2,100,000,000	2.1 billion	America, Australia, Europe, South Africa
Islam	21.43%	1,500,000,000	1.5 billion	Indonesia, Middle East, North Africa, Western Asia
Hinduism	12.86%	900,000,000	0.9 billion	India
Chinese Universalisms	7.14%	500,000,000	0.5 billion	China
Primitive-Indigenous	6.00%	420,000,000	0.42 billion	Africa, America, Asia
Buddhist	5.43%	380,000,000	0.38 billion	China, Eastern Asia
Jewish	0.2%	14,000,000	0.014 billion	Israel, Europe, North America
Other and Nonreligious	16.94%	1,186,000,000	1.186 billion	Worldwide
TOTAL	100%	7,000,000,000	7 billion	Worldwide
Percentages derived from 2005 Wikipedia statistics; populations derived from 2009 Wikipedia statistics				

Christianity is a monotheistic (one God) religion that believes that Jesus Christ is the incarnation of God and savior of humanity. Christ was born of a virgin in a Jewish family in the year 0 BC. He lived only about thirty-three years, worked as a carpenter, preached extensively for his last three years, was crucified, died, was buried, arose from the dead, and ascended into heaven. Christians believe that God exists in three forms: the Father, the Son, and the Holy Spirit. They also believe that those who believe in Christ are forgiven of their sins by grace and will have everlasting life. That's a pretty good deal.

Christianity has as its root the Jewish religion, as does Islam.

Judaism was the first monotheistic religion. Jews can proudly refer to their religion as the first religion proclaiming one and only one God.

The Jewish religion goes back to the time of Abraham, his son Isaac, and Isaac's son Jacob, who reportedly lived about the twentieth century BC. Abraham initially lived in the Euphrates River Valley, present-day Iraq, but moved to Canaan, present-day Israel or Palestine, whichever you prefer. Abraham had two sons; the first son, named Ishmael, was born to Hagar, his mistress. His second son, Isaac, was born to his wife Sarah. Sarah banished Ishmael; but Abraham, Isaac, and Jacob remained to found the Jewish religion.

The Jewish religion is based on the Torah, the first five books of the Bible. Written about 600 BC, the Torah lays down God's laws for living on earth. Little is said about the hereafter. *"From dust you were made, to dust you shall return"* (Gen. 3:19), *"but your spirit returns to God, who gave it"* (Eccles. 12:7). Much is said about the promised land of Israel, the land of Canaan. According to the Torah, God gave the land of Israel to the Jews. Israel is about the size of Vermont. Many Jews believe the land of Israel belongs to them and they are obligated to fight for it. Much of Israel is desert land and not very hospitable. That's not a very good deal.

Islam means "submission" or total surrender of one's self to God. The Islam religion goes back to the twentieth century BC when Abraham's firstborn son, Ishmael, was born to his mistress, Hagar. After Abraham's wife Sarah had her first son, Isaac, Sarah banished Ishmael. After Ishmael grew to manhood, he founded the Islam religion along with his father Abraham. So Islam, Judaism, and Christianity have the same roots.

The prophet Mohammed is regarded as restorer of the original faith founded by Abraham, Moses, Jesus, and other prophets. Muslim means a follower of Islam and the teaching of the prophet Mohammed, who was born in the sixth century. Muslims follow the Qur'an as reportedly revealed to Mohammed by God (Allah) through the angel Gabriel.

Faithful Muslims are required to follow the Five Pillars of Islamic law, rulings regarding virtually all aspects of human life, from dietary laws to warfare. The Five Pillars outline the duties of every Muslim. A minority of Muslims also include a Sixth Pillar of Islamic Law: struggle in the way of God.

There are two basic groups of Muslims, the *Sunni* (85%) and the *Shi'a* (15%). All Muslims follow the Five Pillars of Islamic law: 1) There is none worthy of worship except God; and Mohammed is the messenger of God. 2) Pray five times a day facing toward Mecca, Mohammed's birthplace. 3) Give to others based on the accumulation of wealth. 4) Fast from dawn to dusk during the month of Ramadan (holy month). 5) Make pilgrimage to Mecca at least once in one's lifetime. The Shi'a distinguish between the Greater Jihad, which pertains to religious and moral perfection, and the Lesser Jihad, warfare against persons and states that refuse to submit to the authority of Islam.

Islam teaches that the kingdom of God is a spiritual concept, and that on the Day of Judgment, Allah will judge all mankind based on their deeds. One either goes to heaven or hell, with heaven being the Eternal Kingdom.

Hinduism teaches that the soul is immortal in that it goes on being born and dying over and over again. The soul is reborn because it desires to be reborn to enjoy worldly pleasures. After many births, the soul eventually becomes dissatisfied with the limited happiness the world can bring and begins to seek a higher form of happiness attainable only through spiritual experience. After all desires for the pleasures of the world vanish, the person will not be born again. The immortal soul will then spend eternity absorbed in perfect peace and happiness, knowing that all existence is one and that the immortal soul is part of that existence.

Buddhism teaches reincarnation, a sequence of related lives stretching over a very long time. At the death of one personality, a new one comes into being. Buddhism teaches that what is reborn is not the person but that one moment gives rise to another. It is rare for a person to be reborn in the immediate next life as a human. One may be reborn as a cow or a lama. Other than that, Buddhism stresses the avoidance of unwholesome actions and the cultivation of positive actions. A basic premise is *karma*, or *cause and effect*. Good mental attitudes generate good experiences, while bad mental attitudes generate bad experiences, either of which may be experienced in this life or in a future life.

Confucianism is the main sect of *Chinese Universalists*. *Universalists* include those who apply personal reason and experience to religion, and deny elevation, dogma, and blind faith. Confucianism stresses the importance of education for moral development of the individual. A key concept is that to govern others, one must first govern oneself. There is debate over whether or not Confucianism is actually a religion. It is often referred to as a secular ethical tradition because most religions can be defined as having a God. *Chinese Universalists* more often hold philosophical factual beliefs rather than faith-based beliefs. *Taoist* religions are considered to be the flow of the universe and believe that nature demands proper attitudes, morality, and lifestyle.

Unitarian Universalism is a liberal religion that supports free and responsible search for the truth. Both Unitarians and Universalists have in their origins the Christian faith, but they recognize, appreciate, and value other religions. The extent to which they incorporate particular faiths is a matter of personal choice. Of Christian background, the Unitarian church service is similar to the Christian church service, with Sunday worship, prayer, song, and a sermon. According to the 2000 U.S. census, over 600,000 people identify themselves with the Unitarian Universalist Church, although only about 250,000 are church members.

Atheism believes there is no god.

Agnosticism believes that people cannot rationally determine whether there is or is not a god and that it is pointless to try.

In each of these religions, there are conservative, moderate, and liberal branches. Some of the extremes are militant. They are the ones who get the most publicity from the press and TV journalists. It is the extreme elements that cause the most trouble and conflict in the world. It was that way before the Crusades, and it is still that way today. That is just the nature of religious extremes.

Spiritualists—There are also many who do not partake in any formal religion yet routinely get in touch with their souls. My father was like that. As a child, he was an altar boy in the Episcopal church. As an adult, he never went to church; he did not believe in the virgin birth. But every night he would kneel down at his bed to pray. Daddy knelt there to get in touch with his soul.

Many of us are spiritualists. Many of us spend time trying to get in touch with our souls. I do. And I feel I am successful. But it was not easy to learn how to do that. When I first tried to get in touch with my soul, I got hung up. I got hung up on words I had heard spoken in church—words I thought I knew the meaning of, but obviously did not—simple words like good, bad, evil, Lord, baptism, and grace.

Good sounds like a simple word, but the dictionary lists over thirty definitions for the word good. I prefer the one that says, "Good is anything that is not bad," since *bad* has only over twenty definitions. Good and bad may mean different things to different people.

Evil is more specific than good and bad. *Evil* connotes wicked, sinful, criminal, immoral, foul, vile, horrible, and disgusting things. Any one of these definitions makes something evil.

Lord is the title for God. Christians use the word to mean Jesus Christ, which for many years bothered me because of the First Commandment, "I am thy God. Thou shall have no other God except me." Now I realize and understand that Jesus was God on earth. I often read the Bible, replacing the word *Jesus* with the words *God on earth*. Some think it sacrilege, but it works for me. It cleanses my soul. It is the cleansing of the soul that is all important.

Christians may have different approaches to and different interpretations of the Bible. They vary from such divergent beliefs as, "No man cometh to the kingdom of heaven except through me," to "It doesn't make any difference what we believe as long as we love the environment."

Whatever works is okay with me. Whatever directs our soul that we may meet life's many challenges, whatever settles our soul and makes us happy, whatever cures the diseased soul in preparation for that upcoming journey into eternity is okay with me. But to be okay, it must help us to avoid, or at least minimize, sin.

17 – SIN

Sin is commonly thought of as *knowingly doing wrong*. The issue is, "What is doing wrong?"

Or, for that matter, what is good and what is bad? We can define good as that which is not bad. But there are over twenty definitions of bad. Evil is easier to understand. We recognize evil as wickedness.

We often think about "good and evil." It would be nice if there were definitions of absolute good and absolute evil, but there are not. Good and evil are not absolute. Good and evil depend on the time period and culture at that time. Also, we are all different. None of us think the same. During the Vietnam War, for example, many of us had different views of right and wrong. Furthermore, many of us didn't understand each other's views or even how others could hold such views.

To determine good and bad, philosophers commonly ask two questions: 1) What do people find good, and what do people find bad? 2) What is really good, and what is really bad? The answer to the first question may be ascertained by taking a poll. The answer to the second question may be determined by the use of reasoning.

Aristotle liked to think of right action as the action a person of good character would perform. He felt that *good* has a right and desirable quality and that "good" is whatever produces the best consequences upon the lives of people.

Bad connotes wicked (morally evil and unacceptable), unpleasant (with anger and unpleasantness toward other people), or offensive (likely to cause offense to other people) action.

Evil is wrong or immoral behavior and doing unsatisfactory or hurtful things.

Being raised in a conservative Protestant church, I was taught that sin is sin, no matter what; and that if you accepted Jesus Christ as your personal savior, all your sins would be forgiven. Sin is sin, be it eating too much, lying, coveting your neighbor's wife, or murdering somebody.

Catholics have a much more specific view of sin than Protestants. The Catholic faith lists several levels of sin: mortal sin, venial sin, concupiscence, and eternal sin. All sins, however, are subject to mitigating circumstances, such as mental illness, youth, developmental disorders, and so forth.

Mortal sins are sins of a serious nature, like murder, that cut off the sinner from God's grace (infinite love and mercy). Mortal sin is a rejection of God that, if left to smolder without atonement, will result in eternal punishment in hell. *Atonement* means the ending of the conflict between God and the sinner brought about by the death of Jesus Christ on the cross. Catholics also practice the sacrament of *penance*, meaning confession of sin to a priest and performing devotions imposed by a priest during the sacrament of confession.

Venial sins do not meet the serious levels of mortal sin. Venial sins are relatively minor sins, which do not cut the sinner off from God's grace. The sinner has not been rejected by God. The venial sin is a forgivable sin that must meet any one of three criteria: it does not concern a grave matter, it was not committed with full knowledge, or it was not deliberate and/or was not committed with consent.

Concupiscence denotes a sensuous longing or sexual lust. Protestants teach concupiscence is sin in itself, whereas Catholics teach concupiscence is not sin in itself but is likely to cause sin.

Eternal sin is a sin that cannot be forgiven, a sin where salvation becomes impossible. In the Christian religion, this means speech and blasphemies (vilification) against God.

Historically, mankind has tried to define exactly what sin is. There are over six hundred commandments in the Old Testament Torah alone. Of these, the *Ten Commandments* are recognized as the moral foundation in Judaism, Christianity, and Islam. The Ten Commandments are frequently quoted: 1) Worship no other God than me. 2) Make no idols. 3) Do not use God's name irreverently or swear falsely. 4) Remember the Sabbath and keep it holy. 5) Honor your father and your mother. 6) You must not commit murder. 7) You must not commit adultery. 8) You must not steal. 9) You must not lie. 10) You must not be envious of your neighbor's house or want to sleep with his wife or own anything he has.

Also frequently quoted are the *seven deadly sins* from the book of Proverbs, sins that the Lord hates: 1) Haughty eyes (being arrogant or behaving in a superior way), 2) A lying tongue, 3) Hands that shed innocent blood, 4) A heart that devises wicked plots, 5) Feet that are swift to run into mischief, 6)

A deceitful witness that uttereth lies, and 7) He that soweth discord among brethren.

There is considerable diversity among the world religions concerning mortal sins. For most Christians, mortal sins include such acts as adultery, incest, suicide, murder, robbery, and unnatural carnal sins, such as homosexuality and sodomy. In the Christian faith, each one of these mortal sins makes the soul incapable of eternal bliss until the sinner cleans himself with due repentance. Sin is to know God's will but to intentionally ignore it. For Christians, sin is a state of being that must be atoned for. Judaism is similar, except Judaism teaches that sin is an act, as opposed to a state of being. Hindus and Buddhists, on the other hand, recognize sin as actions that create negative *karma* (actions that determine future state).

Christ, when asked what were the most important commandments, replied: 1) To love God with all thy heart and all thy soul, and 2) To do unto others as you would have them do unto you. These are certainly lofty goals and great challenges in a sinful and competitive world.

18 – MORALITY

"Do unto others as you would have them do unto you." The Golden Rule says it all. There is nothing more to say about morality. So why can't we obey this simple rule?

One answer to that question is because of the multiple circumstances we face in this world. Sometimes we just can't tell what is right and what is wrong. Sometimes things are too complicated to know or even understand the difference between right and wrong. It is sort of like truth: *the nature of truth is untruth,* in that truth depends on the situation. Likewise, some aspects of morality depend on the situation.

What is morality? Is it absolute or relative? Under what conditions must the truth must be told? And under what conditions may truth be concealed? When do we turn the other cheek? When do we demand an eye for an eye?

Morality is the rightness or wrongness of something as judged by established standards. As far back as in the time of Plato, right behavior has been defined as whatever those in power deem it to be. That may sound cruel, but Plato also taught that each of us is an immortal soul, corrupted by vice and purified by virtue or goodness. Plato believed and taught that *private morality is absolute* but *public morality is relative.*

The Jewish Torah, the first five books of the Christian Bible, clearly spells out the basic rules of morality. Thou shall not kill. Thou shall not commit adultery. Thou shall not steal. Thou shall not give false testimony. Thou shall not covet. Few of us can argue with morality as expressed in the Jewish Torah. The rules were clear, and the punishment of disobeying the rules accepted.

Then along came Christianity and the directives "Give unto Caesar that which is Caesar's" and "Turn the other cheek." After that came Machiavelli with "The end justifies the means." So, what are the rules of morality?

Our institutions of higher learning teach that there are two types of morality, public and private. Actually, there are three types of morality—private, public, and political. *Private morality* concerns family and friends. The overriding characteristic of private morality is *love*. Value loved ones: *never, never forsake family.* Friends are for profit or pleasure, but friends come and go. Family is forever.

Public morality concerns normal dealings with other people, such as in the commercial, business world. *Manners* play a major role here because manners provide a close parallel to morality in private life. But there is a pronounced difference between private morality and public morality. In public morality, there are winners and there are losers. In sales, one guy gets the sale, while the other guy loses. In the business world, one team wildly succeeds, while the other team just manages to survive or sometimes is forced out of business by the competition. Sometimes good manners must be accompanied by aggressive but fair competition.

Political morality concerns *conflict*. It may be in the form of business relations, government, or even war. Like wrestling, there are the winners and there are the losers. That is how some conflicts are resolved. Most often, however, *political solutions are compromises*. Deals are cut. Unfortunately, many compromises promote waste, inefficiency, and unfairness. That's just the way compromise is. If you don't like it, don't do it. Just play to win or lose.

So how do we train people for conflict? Well, it starts in school. It starts with report cards. Some kids do better than others. That establishes a pecking order. Those with high grades are considered to have abilities superior to those with low grades. Those with high grades are trained to become leaders. Those with low grades are trained to become followers. Being a follower is not all that bad. In fact, followers are often more happy than leaders. It all has to do with natural talents and training.

Plato taught that music and gymnastics are the basics of all education. Music strengthens the mind; gymnastics strengthens the body.

Music is a developed natural talent that can bring great pleasure. I remember in high school choir, there was a girl with the most beautiful voice. I loved to hear her sing because of the natural talent she possessed. I also remember band. I took up the trombone in the fourth grade along with four of my friends. We would have sectional training with only the trombones. There were five of us. I started out fifth chair. I took private lessons, practiced diligently, and got moved up one step at a time until I was first chair. I felt sort of bad for the other guys but soon got over that because I was good. The others didn't even come close to matching my natural talent. I played first chair in high school. I made first chair in all-state band. When I went to college, I played first chair for four years. Music is fun for the talented. My father played saxophone by ear even though he couldn't read a note of music.

My brother was so talented he had a dance band. Music is fun, but nothing is better than being first chair.

Next comes gymnastics. Gymnastics, like music, belongs to the naturally gifted. At a young age, we can all compete, be it Pop Warner football, Little League baseball, T-ball, or just plain sandlot sports. But as we get older and stronger and enter into organized sports at the high school level, we learn the glory of winning and the agony of defeat. There are winners and losers. There is no middle ground. Ties don't count. When we win, we willingly accept the laurels bestowed upon us. When we lose, we suffer the mental anguish of defeat, failure, and ridicule.

I played football at a small farming town all-white high school. I was starting quarterback for three years. I played every minute of every game, offense and defense. I loved to play football, but I hated the embarrassment of losing. And we lost a lot. Out of twenty-three games, we lost twenty-one, tied one, and won only one. I often look back remembering that period of my life and try to understand what I learned from losing.

There was so much losing that, instead of learning, the experience had an adverse effect on my mental stability. Sometimes I would go home from a losing game and cry with shame in my bed. One time we played an away game at a nearby high school located in an industrial area. We, of course, lost the game. When we walked out of the locker room to get on the bus, we suffered the embarrassment of a huge three-foot-high sign taped along the entire length of the bus. It read *Farmers, go home.* I wanted to rip the sign from the bus, but there were two big muscular black guys standing nearby with their arms folded and their fists clinched. We just got on the bus and let the coach rip the sign off. I have always regretted that I didn't have the courage to rip it off myself. But I was a trombone player. I didn't want to lose my teeth.

So, what did I learn about morality from these gymnastic experiences of organized sports? Well, first of all, I leaned how to *lose gracefully* on the outside and suffer quietly on the inside. Second, I learned to *play by the rules,* the rules of those in power. And third, I learned that the rules of combat on the football field need not apply to our personal lives; what happens on the football field should stay on the football field. *Never let your public life interfere with your personal life.*

That is how we are trained in school to compete, to deal with conflict. Most of us also receive training from our family. I distinctly remember my father telling me at a young age, "Don't ever start a fight; but if you get into one, finish it." Well, I never did start a fight, but I did get into one. I finished it lying on my back with the other guy pinning me to the floor so tightly that I couldn't get up. I never told Dad about that fight, but I often wonder if he would have been proud that I finished it.

So, after all of this training on how to deal with conflict, we enter the world as adults to find there are established rules of conflict, just as there are established rules of football. The Golden Rule governs personal morality: *"Do unto others what you would have them do unto you"*; if you don't, you will end up with no friends. Laws of the land govern public morality; if you don't obey them, you will end up in jail. These are the basic black and white principles of moral behavior, but there are many shades of gray.

How do we, as teenagers and young adults, make the moral decisions that will affect the rest of our lives? How do we select and treat our lovers?

The teenage years are particularly difficult in that we are adults in training. We make mistakes. We are allowed to make mistakes. At that time of our lives, we learn by trial and error. Our hope is that we will not irreparably damage our psyche, our reputation, or our health. As young people, we have to choose between lifestyles. Who do we hang with? Into what environments do we allow ourselves to wander? How do we handle temptation? Do we live lives of sexual moderation or of sexual promiscuity? I chose the former. My high school sweetheart was captain of the girls' virginity team, and her mother was the coach. I followed my father's wise advice to stay away from prostitutes. And when I finally found the love of my life, I married her and always remained faithful to her. Growing up is just part of life. We all get through it, one way or another. We must be careful the direction we start out in, because chances are, *the direction we start in is where we will probably end up.*

The era of youth ends at age eighteen. At age eighteen, we can be tried in a court of law as adults. There is no more forgiveness for childish mistakes. If we screw up after age eighteen, we pay a hefty price. Today, over two million Americans are behind bars for everything from murder to petty larceny. The rule of criminal law sets our moral standards as a society. For the most part, criminal law is fair and just. But it has not always been so.

In the past, some standards of criminal law were political and varied from place to place, from state to state, and from nation to nation. I have in my home library a copy of the 1852 *Laws of the State of Delaware*. In it I was astounded to read the punishments for free Negros and mulattos were more severe than for white persons. In addition, no free Negro or mulatto could vote at elections, be elected, or be appointed to any office of trust. Times change, and so does legislated morality. Thank God we were not raised in those tumultuous days of incivility.

We all look back in anger at World War II. How could Adolf Hitler have ever caused the Holocaust? I was certain I could never act in such an irresponsible manner—and then came Vietnam.

Those of you who read *Noble Conflict* will recognize the terrible guilt I feel because I killed a man. The killing was uncalled for. It was unnecessary. But it happened. The justification I used was that I did what I was trained to do. That makes it right. In wartime, we don't do what is morally right; *we do what we are trained to do.* That's the way it is. That's the way it has to be.

What moral standards do we use to select our careers? How do we behave in professional situations? How do we treat our employers, our coworkers, and our clients? How do we deal with those whose moral standards are different from ours?

Then, finally, I settled down to a regular job, my wife had a baby, and we bought a house. I didn't have to think much about job security because the bosses handed down plenty of work. Life was good. Then the business cycle changed, the old bosses left, and I had to fend for myself. For the most part, I did what the new bosses wanted. My father-in-law once told me that *if you do what the bosses want, you will be all right.*

For most of us, our public morality closely parallels our private morality. We do our job. We don't cause any trouble. And at the end of the workweek, we take our paycheck and go home. We happily do what we are told until we feel threatened by loss of the job, by disrespect from others, or by having to do things that are against our accepted morals. When backed into a corner, we fight. We fight those whom we perceive to threaten us.

Plato taught that the morals of those in power are not the same as private morality. Those in power sometimes find it necessary to hurt others, to lie, and to cheat to attain the higher good. Even today, colleges teach and train students in Machiavellian strategy and tactics—the end justifies the means. Conflicts are unavoidable. We may sometimes ask the question "What is proper public morality for each of us under the given circumstances?"

I have spent much of my professional career navigating in the world of public morality. I wrote a lot of professional proposals. In the engineering business, you have to write about ten unsuccessful proposals to get one accepted. Competition is usually thought of as the accepted mode to select what is best, or what is supposedly best. For years I wrote detailed project proposals that, from my viewpoint at least, were pretty good. It was difficult and frustrating when they were rejected, but I survived. The problem was that, for the most part, a good proposal is not enough to get the job. You must also have your political bases covered. You have to know the right people and give them what they want. If the game is pay for play, that's the way it is. Don't participate in it. You will only get hurt. *Let others do the dirty work.*

Do a little something else to whip your competition. Usually, you have to know somebody. Then, that somebody has to like you and want you. The tough part is to get a good and honorable point man. The point man, the contact man, the presenter, is key to success.

I have observed that the presenter must be of a likable nature, good looking, articulate, and smart. The presenter must be able to sort out and remember what is said at meetings with the potential clients. Not many of us have those characteristics, and at the same time have the necessary talent and perseverance to do the work. It's like in car sales. You buy from somebody who is likable but who undoubtedly could never design or build a car.

What did I learn at work? *Always be professional.* And always be unapologetic about it. Even in defeat, we are always viewed with respect when we abide by sound personal moral standards and by the ethical standards of our profession.

Each of us must decide what our personal moral standards will be. They should never be violated, no matter what—even when we have to do what we are trained to do, even when we live by standards of professional ethics designed to protect the profession, even though we stand to gain at another's loss. *Never, never violate personal morals.*

19 – PROFESSIONAL ETHICS

We all deal with professionals at sometime in our lives. When doing so, we need to know and understand where they are coming from. We need to know exactly what they are expected to do and what their ethical responsibility is to us, to the public, and to their profession. The nature of professional ethics may surprise you.

Professional ethics are the moral principles governing the appropriate conduct of a group of professional people, such as lawyers, engineers, or medical doctors. Ideally, professional ethics should be drafted to protect the public. In reality, however, they are also designed to protect the profession.

Doctors pledge to provide competent medical care with compassion and respect, to respect the patient's rights and maintain privacy, to hold paramount responsibility to the patient, to continue lifelong professional study, and to support access to medical care for all people. They do, however, except in emergencies, maintain freedom to choose who to serve, who to associate with, and in what environment to practice. Unfortunately, doctors are also chased around by lawyers.

Lawyers are officers of the court. Lawyers pledge to represent the client zealously within boundaries of the law, to preserve confidence and secrets of the client, to exercise independent professional judgment on behalf of the client, and to avoid the appearance of improprieties. Lawyers are always involved in conflict. That is what they get paid for. No conflict, no need for lawyers. But conflict is stressful. Statistics show law is one of the most stressful and depressing occupations.

Engineers pledge to hold paramount the safety, health, and welfare of the public, to perform services only in their area of competence, to issue statements in an objective and truthful manner, and to avoid conflicts of interest. They also pledge a zero tolerance for bribery, fraud, and corruption, and to not compete unfairly with others. Those goals are usually easy to meet for the average engineer because the average engineer is not in the business of engineering. I know a little about engineering ethics. I spent my engineering career working for a firm of consulting engineers. Consulting firms are notorious for burning out their employees with long hours and little variety. Most engineers have to take it, but I was lucky. When my work ran out, I retrained on the job in other specialties. For the most part, I found engineering fun but the business of engineering awful.

Teachers pledge to act with honesty and integrity, to ensure the safety and welfare of their students, to respect confidential information of the students, and to not discriminate. They also pledge to not assist or counsel any person who is not a registered teacher, and to never teach while under the influence. I don't know why they have to pledge that, but that's the way it is. Most teachers who keep their nose clean and their teaching skills up, enjoy a good and secure life with excellent benefits.

Pastors pledge to hold trust in traditions, to maintain a disciplined and wholesome lifestyle, to recognize that their primary obligation is to the church, and to observe the sanctity of confidentiality except in the case of perceived life-threatening or substantial harm. The ministry is a most ethical profession in that ministers pledge to strive to preserve the dignity, maintain the discipline, and promote the integrity of the vocation. Most pastors do, however, preach their own interpretation of biblical truth. And some are secretively arrogant and aggressive.

Soldiers traditionally pledge to be prepared to give their life in the defense of their country; to never surrender of their own free will; that if captured, to continue to resist by all means available and make every effort to escape; that if taken prisoner of war, to keep the faith and when questioned, to give only name, rank, service number, and date of birth; to make no oral or written statements disloyal to their country and its allies or harmful to their cause; to remain dedicated to the principles that made this country free; and to trust in God and their country. Contemporary pledges include loftier but less definitive goals and specific codes of conduct for such things as recruit training and serving in countries where contact is made with civilians of unknown persuasion. Most of the contemporary codes of conduct offer confusing and often unachievable objectives that cannot be met even by career soldiers, let alone eighteen- and nineteen-year-olds, who make up the vast majority of people in our frontline military forces.

Psychotherapists are among the most poorly treated professionals. Insurance companies and lawyers interfere with psychiatric treatment of the patient. Insurance companies limit the amount they pay for counseling services, and lawyers get rich with bitter divorce suits because it is often easiest and cheaper for the psychotherapist to recommend divorce rather than save a marriage. Also, rules stressing unreasonable concerns regarding the civil rights of patients have led to results counterproductive to family life. In addition, measures that pretend to protect the welfare of the patient, such as not talking to family members, not allowing duplication of written reports, limited computerization, or private data banks, in many cases actually are not in the best interest of the patient but in the best interest of lawyers and insurance companies.

Businessmen, for the most part, do not enjoy the status of the licensed professional. Business motives are thought to be less noble than those of licensed professionals, although in many cases they are not. It is profit that determines if the businessman survives. Business managers are defined by one and only one obligation—to maximize profits for the stockholders. This unflattering image is developed by the brightest and best graduates of the country's most prestigious business schools where MBAs are reportedly trained to fire old men and outsource jobs overseas. Business life is competitive, but it doesn't need to be unfair. It is shared values that hold our culture together. A job is never just a job. It has a moral dimension. When corporate values conflict with personal values, we must make a decision as to which path to follow. But *when the demands of business duty conflict with the well-being of society, it is the business that must yield.* That is the ultimate business ethic.

Politicians have but limited ethical goals—*don't break any man-made laws, don't betray allies, and maintain a good public image.* Other than that, out of necessity to survive, they must sometimes demonstrate immoral behavior. In order to win a battle, they will often conceal important facts, tell half-truths, and even lie. Political students are trained by our colleges and universities in Machiavellian strategies and tactics. Political necessity sometimes requires the overriding of personal morality to have a decisively positive outcome representing the best and highest common good. Politics, by nature, involves conflict. Without conflict, there is no need for politics. All is fair in love and war and politics.

Artisans possess the best ethics of all—*learn from the best, become the best, produce the best.*

20 – SCIENCE

Many of us start out in life choosing a career path without ever knowing what career paths are out there. Many lucrative professional careers follow scientific paths—paths of training in natural science, social and behavioral science, applied science, and interdisciplinary science. These paths sound interesting, but they take a certain amount of natural talent and hard work to master. Also, there is great disparity in income among these careers. Before selecting one, you might want to conduct a cost study and a supply and demand analysis.

Scientific careers are based on knowledge and practices capable of producing a reasonably predictable outcome. You get paid for knowledge-based practice. People will hire you for knowledge-based practice that guarantees them a certain procedure, even when the outcome is not necessarily good. The patient may die, but the doctor does his best with the knowledge he has.

There are three broad categories of science: natural science, social science, and mathematics. A separate chapter is devoted to mathematics because of its importance and complexity.

Natural science studies rules and laws of nature: astronomy, biology, chemistry, earth science, and physics. *Social science* studies social groups and human society: anthropology, criminology, economics, geography, history, political science, psychology, and sociology.

Of course, there are many subcategories of each, but all study of science is directed toward applied science: computer science; engineering; health science, such as bioengineering, dentistry, health care, medicine, nursing, and pharmacy; and social work.

Then there are the related sciences, such as biomedical engineering, environmental studies, library and informational studies, forestry, urban planning, and of course, history and philosophy of science and the scientific method. Notice how the above lists include the hard sciences, those demanding more skill, as well as the casual sciences, those that are interesting but of little practical value. How else could colleges and universities fill up their classrooms?

Everybody has a right to an education, even though there is little or no demand for their skills. Be careful selecting a career choice. Great injustices have been done by directing students to expensive educations that promise few financial rewards but big student loans.

Natural Science

All *natural science* is based on the *scientific method*, where scientists collect observable evidence, record measurable data, and analyze the information. The data are then hypothesized into a theoretical explanation of how things work, experimentally tested, and then published so that other scientists can review and confirm or refute the findings.

Prior to the sixteenth century, the study of knowledge was called philosophy. In fact, in the time of Socrates, Plato, and Aristotle, the study and development of all knowledge was called philosophy. There was no such terminology as science. It was only in the Age of Enlightenment that people started to recognize what science really is—*knowledge based on the scientific method.*

Scientific theory is unprovable. Unlike mathematics, scientific theory is always open to falsification as new evidence is presented. This is not always good. People learn given scientific theories like the *Bohr model of the atom*, a simple model of electrons rotating around a nucleus. This Bohr model helps us to easily understand and manage chemistry and physics. Then somebody comes along and proposes the quantum theory, with its quarks and quacks, and other theories such as antimatter. The old-timers are suddenly out of favor and have to retrain. But then how else can colleges and universities fill up their classrooms?

Social Science

Social science is the study of human behavior and societies. Social science is based upon the knowledge of basically positive experiences. Social science avoids the negative. Unlike natural science, social science is neither based on theory nor is predictable. The major branches of social science are: anthropology, economics, education (including geography and history), law, linguistics, political science, public administration, psychology, clinical psychology, social work, and sociology.

Anthropology is the holistic science of man. Holism means "whole." It implies that components of a system cannot be explained by its component parts alone. Anthropology is concerned with all human beings across time and places and with *all aspects of man* (cultural, economic, ecological, and psychological).

Economics describes the production, distribution, and consumption of *wealth*. *Microeconomics* concentrates on the individual unit—the person, the household, the industry. *Macroeconomics* studies an economy as a whole.

Education encompasses learning and teaching skills, as well as the imparting of knowledge, judgment, and wisdom. *Geography* examines both the physical and human phenomena related to the earth, the oceans, and the climate. *History* is a narrative of the past. History is sometimes more fiction than fact because it is written with prejudice.

Laws are *enforceable rules* made up by politicians. Law is part of economics because any laws about common tort (civil wrongdoing), property laws, labor laws, and tax and business laws have lasting and long-term effects on the distribution of wealth.

Linguistics is the study of language. It pertains to the cognitive (thought processes) and social impacts of language.

Political science deals with the theory of politics (theory and practices of government, and power relationships among people, groups, and organizations) and political systems, practices, and behavior.

Public administration is devoted to the development, implementation, and study of branches of government.

Psychology includes the study of the human mind, characteristics of mental makeup, and subtle manipulative behavior.

Clinical psychology relates to the assessment and treatment of mental problems.

Social work trains specialists in work with individuals, families, groups, organizations, and communities.

Sociology is the study of society and human social activities.

Applied Science

Applied science is where the money is, or at least where it is supposed to be. Those of us in the professions often wonder exactly where the money went. It certainly didn't go to me. I worked most of my lifetime for a small firm of consulting engineers as a project engineer/project manager. I designed water and wastewater treatment plants, highway bridges, and small dams. For most of my early career, I felt like and was treated like a professional. Then big business came along. All of a sudden, instead of being called a professional engineer, I was referred to as a profit center. Somehow we lost control of our profession.

I now even feel sorry for medical doctors. Even our most dedicated doctors are at the mercy of lawyers, politicians, and bean-counting insurance companies. Important *medical* disciplines include: anesthesiology (airway management to keep patients stable during trauma), cardiology (heart and major blood vessels), clinical laboratory services (diagnostic laboratories), dermatology (skin), emergency medicine (hospital), endocrinology (hormones, diabetes, and thyroid), family medicine, gastroenterology (digestion and tube passage from mouth to anus), surgery, geriatrics (old people), hematology (blood), hepatology (liver), infectious disease, intensive care (life support), nephrology (kidneys), neurology (nervous systems), obstetrics (female reproduction), oncology (cancer), ophthalmology (visual), orthopedic surgery (musculoskeletal), otolaryngology (ear, nose, and throat), palliative care (pain), pathology (clinical examination of tissues and body fluids), physical medicine and rehabilitation, plastic surgery (cosmetic and reconstructive), proctology (rectum, anus, and colon), psychiatry (cognitive perceptual, emotional, and behavioral), pulmonology (respiratory system), radiology (imaging and diagnostics), rheumatology (joints), and urology (urinary tract).

I have the highest regard for doctors, even though I was once misdiagnosed with sarcoidosis when I really had cancer. The first doctor I went to gave me a needle biopsy, which came back negative. The second doctor decided to cut into me to see what he could find. While I lay on the operating table, my surgeon was arguing on the phone with my insurance company. Finally my doctor told the insurance company, *"You are interfering with my treatment of the patient."* That did it. The insurance company then allowed the operation.

Other *applied sciences* include such things as computer science (IT or information technology), engineering (aeronautical, biomedical, chemical, civil, computer, electrical, fire-protection, genetic, mechanical, military, mining, and nuclear), and health sciences (health care, bioengineering, dentistry, epidemiology—study of disease, medicine, nursing, and pharmacy).

The study of science is so important to society that universities offer degrees in natural science, social science, and applied science. At the bachelor level, there are *bachelor of arts* (general knowledge rather than specialization) and *bachelor of science* (more specialization on a particular science and less of a broader education). Today, degrees are also offered in various fields of applied science, such as bachelor of civil engineering (very specialized technical training but little or no social science).

Whether to pursue a master's degree immediately after receiving a bachelor's degree often depends on how much money you have and whether or not you are offered a good job. When offered a good job, many take the job. The ideal time to seek the master's degree is after working for a while. Try to get out in the workplace and find out what's happening out there before you start to specialize too much. The one thing that screws things up is marriage and babies. When baby needs a new pair of shoes, work comes before education. You will eventually study anyway, because learning and self-improvement are lifetime jobs.

21 – MATHEMATICS

Some of you may be tempted to skip this chapter. It may look tough, but it's not. Some of you may find it all too elementary to bother reading, but even you can benefit from occasionally reviewing the basics. Even you may have forgotten something. Even you may need to talk mathematics with your children or your grandchildren. All mathematics is simply add, subtract, multiply, and divide. The rest is secret language, proven shortcuts, and rational thinking.

Every mathematical problem boils down to the basics—*add, subtract, multiply, and divide.* You can calculate in your head, use your fingers, or count matchsticks. You can calculate using the numerous definitions and shortcuts developed over the years. You can use a calculator or a computer. But to do any mathematics, you must know the basics taught to every schoolchild: add, subtract, multiply, and divide. If you don't know how to do that, you cannot survive independently in society.

Algebra
The first step after the basics is *algebra*. Although some math teachers make it hard to understand, algebra is really very simple. Algebra is simply developing equations and solving for unknowns. There is only one rule: you need *one equation for every unknown*. Once you have all of the equations, you substitute, simplify, and solve by adding, subtracting, multiplying, and dividing. The trick is to accurately develop the equations, and to achieve that you have to *think logically.*

Geometry
The next tier is *geometry*, the mathematics of two-dimensional shapes, and three-dimensional shapes. In this field there are two important concepts to

understand: the *Pythagorean Theorem* and *pi (π)*, pronounced pie. A *theorem* is a statement of logic that is provable.

The Pythagorean Theorem applies to all right triangles, all triangles with one ninety-degree angle. The *Pythagorean Theorem* states, *"The square of the hypotenuse equals the sum of the squares of the other two sides."* This theorem is profound in that any straight line figure may be divided into right triangles, thereby allowing for solution of the whole or any part.

The other profound theorem of geometry applies to circles. The theorem of pi states that the *circumference of a circle = π times the diameter = 2 π* times the radius. Pi is an irrational number; it cannot be expressed as an exact fraction. That means it is an infinitely long fraction. The value of pi to five decimal places is *π = 3.14159.*

Both of these concepts were known to the ancient Egyptians, Greeks, and Romans. Archimedes (250 BC) and Liu Hui (AD 265) proved the theorem of pi. The Greek philosopher Pythagoras (500 BC) is generally given credit for the Pythagorean Theorem, although it was also known to the Babylonians, the Asians, and God knows who else.

All of these guys pictured their geometric works in two dimensions, with points plotted as referenced from two intersecting lines. These lines intersect at right angles to each other. Points are plotted as horizontal values (say, x) and vertical values (say, y).

This is the same way we picture geometry today. Two-dimensional geometry is called *plane geometry.* Three-dimensional geometry is called *solid geometry.* For solid geometry, simply add another axis line (say, z), passing through and at right angles to the intersection of the x-y axis. Plane geometry has two axes: x and y. Solid geometry has three axes: x, y, and z.

Every student of geometry must master the simple *parabola* ($y = x^2$), the simple *hyperbola* ($x^2 - y^2 = 1$), the simple *ellipse* ($x^2 + y^2 = 1$), and the simple *exponential curve* ($y = a^x$). Constants may be included in each of these equations, but it is easiest to first understand the basics without the constants.

Trigonometry

Trigonometry is the next step up. *Trigonometry deals with triangles,* particularly those formed within a circle. Trigonometry entails the development of defined properties and relationships of right triangles. Trigonometry consists of a system of definitions and shortcuts to solve geometric problems; the most important are *sine* (opposite/hypotenuse), *cosine* (adjacent/hypotenuse), and *tangent* (opposite/adjacent).

There are *360 degrees in a circle*, 180 degrees in a half circle, and 90 degrees in a quarter of a circle.

Radians are another measure of angle. One *radian* is the angle subtended by an arc that is equal in length to the radius of the circle. Since the circumference of a circle = $2\pi r$ and since the arc length of one radian is r, there must be 2π radians in one revolution. And since there are 360 degrees in a circle, one radian is equal to $360/2\pi$, or about 57.2958 degrees. Radians are used in calculus instead of degrees because the radian is a pure number. It needs no symbol.

All of the above disciplines—algebra, geometry, and trigonometry—are included in basic high school education. Everybody should take these subjects, but it is surprising how many students are reluctant to do so because they think they are too hard. These subjects are not difficult. It is only the teachers and textbooks that make them difficult. Those students who learn, learn because they are provided with good study material and they have good teachers and mentors who take an interest in them. Everyone should be able to enjoy algebra, geometry, and trigonometry.

Calculus

Calculus is the mathematics of change. It's *rocket science*. It's a system of calculation guided by symbolic manipulations of expressions. In other words, it is hard to comprehend. It is difficult to comprehend because of the traditional way it has been taught.

I took college calculus for two years. While I apparently gleaned enough knowledge to pass the tests, I never really understood the subject. I never knew why I was doing what I was doing. Pure mathematics was apparently not my thing.

As a matter of fact, I never ever had to use calculus in my professional career, except for those times when it was buried within a computer program. But there are those who do use it, such as aeronautical engineers calculating the trajectory path of rockets whose weight and fuel load vary. Some others may use it to make preliminary gross estimates. Still others may use it in computer software. But, in general, calculus is not for the average line engineer. Calculus is more akin to rocket science. Academia loves it. It's a perfect way to conceal what they know—or don't know—and a perfect way to force two thirds of engineering students out of engineering.

Function

My first difficulty with calculus began with the word *function*. Beginning on the first day in class, the professor, a PhD, used the word *function* to explain what he was talking about. He apparently thought we all knew what he meant by *function*. I didn't. I looked around me at the three hundred freshman students in the lecture hall thinking everybody else knew something I did not. And, since it was a lecture, I could not ask any questions.

Several days after the lecture, we met in groups of about twenty, each with a graduate student instructor. But since the instructor was a graduate student and since I didn't want to look stupid in front of my classmates, I was afraid to ask any questions. So finally I thought of looking up the word *function* in the dictionary. The dictionary lists over fifteen meanings of the word *function*.

In two years of college calculus, I learned practically nothing. Then, much later in life, I studied calculus on my own. I bought a couple modern-day calculus books and was astounded to see how complicated they still were. I finally concluded there are only two *important procedures* in calculus—*differentiation and integration*. In order to perform either of these two procedures, you need a function. Something must vary according to something else. If it doesn't, you don't use calculus; you have to plot it on charts and graphs to see what's going on. So if you want to use calculus, you must have an equation, which defines a function.

Before we go any further, there is some other basic information you need. First, you have to know the Greek alphabet. For some reason, mathematicians love to use Greek letters to symbolize unknowns. This tends to confuse the casual reader.

The Greek Alphabet

Greek Letter	Greek Name	English Equivalent
A α	Alpha	a
B β	Beta	b
Γ γ	Gamma	g
Δ δ	Delta	d
E ε	Epsilon	ĕ
Z ζ	Zeta	z
H η	Eta	ē
θ ϴ	Theta	th
I ι	Iota	i
K κ	Kappa	k
Λ λ	Lambda	l
M μ	Mu	m
N ν	Nu	n
Z ε	Xi	x
O o	Omicron	ŏ
Π π	Pi	p

Pρ	Rho	r
Σσ	Sigma	s
Ττ	Tau	t
Tν	Upsilon	u
Φǿ	Phi	ph
Xχ	Chi	ch
Ψψ	Psi	ps
Ωι	Omega	ō

Second, there are a few important symbols you need to know to understand the language of advanced mathematics.

<u>Symbol Name</u>   <u>Function</u>

x and y Variables   Choose one variable to derive from the other.

$y = x^2$ Equation   Derive y from x.

f(x)   *Function* of x   That which determines y, say, *x*.

df(x)/dx *Derivative*   *Rate of change*, slope of line, say *y/x*, at given x.

$\int_a^b$ f(x)dx *Integral*   *Area under the x-y curve* between x = a and x = b

The graph of the function may be a straight line, such as y = 2x. Or it may be a curved line, such as $y = 4\,x^2$. Or it may be a discontinuous line, such as y = tan x. (Tangent ninety degrees = 1/0 = infinity.) Any number divided by zero equals infinity. To plot the graph, just plug in a few values of x, calculate the corresponding values of y, and plot the results on a piece of graph paper. Remember, in calculus, f(x) = y means y is a function of x.

Differentiation

Differentiation gives you the rate of change or the slope of the graph at any desired point. It is very simple to find the derivative of any *polynomial* expression (a sum of terms, each of which contains a constant and variables raised to a positive power). *To differentiate polynomial equations, bring the power to the front and then reduce the exponent by one.* So the deferential of f(x) = y is 1. This means the slope of the line is 1, or 1/1. The slope of the function line is the opposite over the adjacent, y/x. For f(x) = 3x, the slope = 3, or 3/1. The function curve is a straight line.

For f(x) = x^2, a curved function, differentiate by bringing the exponent to the front and then reduce the original exponent by one, or df(x)/dx = 2x. At x = 1, the slope of the line is 2. At x = 2, the slope of the line is 4. At x = 3, the slope of the line is 6. The derivative is the slope of the line at the point of interest.

So, let's prove that it works. To do that, it is necessary to know one important mathematical relationship: $(a + b)^2 = (a^2 + 2ab + b^2)$. That's just the way it is.

Now, to calculus explained. The slope of a straight line is y/x. But what is the slope of the line y = x^2? Well, let's see. The slope varies at every point on the curve. So calculus says take a very small portion of the line, such as a small portion of x, or Δx, and a corresponding portion of y, or Δy, and find out what that slope is. The slope of the line is dy/dx over a very short interval.

$$dy/dx = \frac{(x+\Delta x)^2 - x^2}{\Delta x} = \frac{(x^2 + 2x\Delta x + \Delta x^2) - x^2}{\Delta x} = \frac{2x\,\Delta x + \Delta x^2}{\Delta x} = 2x + \Delta x$$

Since Δx is small, it may be ignored. And dy/dx = 2x.

You could derive lots of other derivatives, but why bother? They have already been derived for us and are listed in standard mathematical tables.

Then there is the second derivative. The *second derivative* is the rate of change of the rate of change. The second derivative is simply the derivative of the first derivative. For f(x) = x^2, the second derivative is 2. That means the rate of change changes by 2 every time the value of x changes by 1.

Integration

Next comes integration. *Integration is the area under the x-y curve between two limits* (two points along the x axis, from here to there). To find the integral, merely take the *antiderivative* (reverse the process) and then solve that equation at each of the limits. Then subtract the value at the lower limit from the value at the upper limit.

The integral is commonly designated by the symbol $\int_a^b$ (fx). *To integrate a polynomial* equation (sum of a number of terms, each of which may consist of a constant and variables raised to a positive power), simply *increase the power by one and then divide by the new power.* Calculate the value at the upper limit and subtract from it the value at the lower limit. The result is the area under the original function curve between these two limits. For simplicity, we will assume the lower limit is 0. That means all of the following plots start at x = 0 and y = 0. And all plots along the x axis end at x = 3.

If f(x) = x, then $_0\int^3 f(x)\, dx = \frac{1}{2} x^2 = 4.5$, or the area of a triangle with base = 3 and height = 3; or ½ width × height = 3 × 3/2 = 4.5.

If f(x) = 2x, then $_0\int^3 2x = 2 \times 3^2/2 = 9$, or the area of a triangle with base x = 3 and height y = 6; or ½ × 3 × 6 = 9.

For f(x) = $3x^2$, then $_0\int^3 3x^2 = 3 \times 3^3/3 = 27$, or the area under a parabola with base = 3 and height = 27, or 1/3 base × height = 3 × 27/3 = 27.

Integration works because of the provable basic theorem of calculus: *The area under a continuous derivative curve between two limits is equal to the rise in the function curve between the same two limits.* That's amazing, simply amazing. And it can be proven graphically.

Other

And that's about it for the basics. Of course, there are several other things to know. First, when you integrate, you must add the constant C if your curve does not start at x = 0 and y = 0 to find out where your function curve crosses the y axis at x = 0. If you take a test, be sure to add the constant C, or you may fail the test. But you really don't have to because in integration between two limits, C is merely subtracted from C.

Advanced mathematics uses logarithms and exponents to define certain functions.

Logarithms and exponents are related as follows: if $b^y = x$, then *b is the base and y is the log.* You may use any base you want. The two most common bases are *log base 10* and *natural log to the base e.* In engineering, the designation commonly used is *common logarithm, log_{10}, or simply log.* The power designates how many times to multiply by 10, a concept easily recognizable to practically anybody.

In statistics and economics, the expression commonly used is *exponential logarithm, Log_e, ln, log, or Ln,* where *e = 2.71828.* So when $e^x = y$, y log_e = x, where e is the base and x is the exponential function. The exponential function is represented as e^x, or how many times e must be multiplied times itself to equal y. So goes accounting. All you really need is a good set of *interest tables* to tell you the banks are stealing your money by taking it from you, collecting interest from somebody else, but paying you little or no interest on your investment.

You can learn how to derive these theorems by studying calculus. A word about the differentiation and integration of exponential functions and trigonometric functions—they are tricky to derive. For those who are interested, $d(e^x)/dx = e^x$; $d(\sin)/dx = \cos x$; $d(\cos x)/dx = -\sin x$; and $d(\tan x)/dx = (1/\sin x)^2$. You can derive all kinds of derivatives and integrals, but it is very time-consuming.

The study of calculus can quickly become very laborious. Also, mathematicians love the subject so much they may carry instruction beyond the point of diminishing returns. Formal education in advanced mathematics seems to include a mire of coded messages, meant only for the educated to understand. You may spend much of your time learning how given functions are differentiated and integrated. Fortunately, there are many *published standard mathematical tables* to refer to for formulas of various functions. These include such things as formulas for the areas of various geometric shapes and for interest tables.

The basics of calculus are simple, but the actual calculus soon becomes very complicated. Just remember, all you are really doing is finding the slope of the function line and the area under the function line between two limits. The study of calculus is laborious, with many dark alleys. You may find some of it valuable, but much of it you will not. The important thing about studying calculus is the mental exercise. It exercises the brain. But it is very hard work. After each study interval, you deserve time to relax and rest your brain.

Mathematics is serious work. Accuracy is needed to properly project the trajectory of speeding rockets, with changing fuel weight, acceleration, and velocity, that put men on the moon. The Euler Buckling formula was needed to predict the World Trade Center collapse when those flimsy little floor trusses quickly heated up to fail in providing lateral support to the main columns. Miscalculations, design oversights, and faulty algorithms (problem-solving procedures) lead to monumental disasters; but accurate calculations, sound oversight, and proper design procedures lead to marvelous accomplishments.

22 – MATTER, ENERGY, AND SPACE-TIME

Those of you with little interest in science may not want to read this chapter because it takes some study and a little deep thought. Some of you will read and understand it quickly. Some of you may take days to get through it. Some of you may never get through it. Nevertheless, it is essential to at least appreciate the concepts of matter, energy, and space-time because those concepts have great spiritual connotations.

This chapter is about the natural laws of nature. Natural laws are the very nature and person of God himself. *"I remain the same yesterday, today, and forever."*

Matter

So, what is this "stuff" called *matter*? It has mass and occupies space. It is directly associated with the weight of a given object. And it exhibits the property of inertia—when at rest it tends to stay at rest; when moving it tends to keep moving in the same direction at the same speed. And it can be converted to energy. Matter can exist in three basic states: solids, gas, and liquids. Plus, for those of you who are interested, other states exist at the quantum level (indivisible entity level).

Every schoolchild knows of the theory that all matter is made up of basic atoms, which consist of a positively charged nucleus about which spin negatively charged electrons. The outer electrons can be removed or added to. When this happens, the atoms become charged because of the unbalance of electrons and protons. Charged particles attract oppositely charged particles and repel like charged particles. The *atom* is the smallest entity of any particular matter (water, iron, hydrogen, etc.)

The weight of the atom depends on the number of protons and neutrons in the nucleus. The *nucleus* consists of positively charged *protons* and *neutrons* (protons with no charge). The total number of electrons in an atom will equal the total number of protons. The like charged particles are held together by the strongest force in nature—the *strong nuclear force*, a force one million billion billion billion billion times the force of gravity, a force so strong that even alchemists can't turn iron into gold.

Electrons circle the nucleus at high speeds. In some cases they travel near the speed of light, in other cases much less than the speed of light. Each electron is located on one of seven orbits, or energy levels, depending on the total number of electrons and the energy level of the atom. When the outer electron shell is not full, that atom wants to take free electrons (which makes it negatively charged), to give up electrons (which makes it positively charged), or to share electrons with one or more other atoms (which makes it part of a molecule).

When an atom absorbs energy (such as from heat), some electrons move to an inner shell. When energy is given off, electrons move to an outer shell. In both cases, energy is absorbed or emitted as electromagnetic energy.

According to the "big bang theory" for creation of the universe, all atoms were created only in the first few moments of creation because it takes a great amount of energy to form the nuclear bond. These atoms are defined in the *periodic table of the elements* by atomic number. *Atomic number* is the total of all protons. They are listed horizontally by group (atoms with similar properties) and vertically by period (number of electron shells filled). There are a total of one hundred eighteen different types of atoms listed in eighteen groups and seven periods. Ninety-two of these elements are naturally occurring. *Atomic weight* is the sum of all protons plus all neutrons (uncharged protons) plus all electrons. Atomic weight is important in evaluating chemical reactions with other elements.

Chemistry is the study of the electrons and electron behavior. *Nuclear physics* is the study of the nucleus of the atom.

The *molecule* is the smallest part of a chemical compound. A molecule is an electrically neutral group of at least two atoms held together by strong chemical bonds. Strong chemical bonds are formed by *sharing or transferring electrons between atoms*. Molecules then bond together by strong molecular bonds, such as sharing of free electrons (metallic bonds); or by sharing electrons between atoms (covalent bonds); or by weak molecular bonds of magnetic attraction, such as hydrogen bonds like the bipolar bonds of water molecules. The nature of all materials (strength, ductility, etc.) is dependent upon the type of molecules, the type of molecular bonds, and temperature and pressure.

There are four important facts concerning molecules: 1) All matter is composed of tiny particles called molecules. 2) There are spaces between these molecules. 3) The molecules are constantly moving. 4) Molecules attract each other.

Molecules bond together to form the stuff we call matter—stuff like rocks, sand, water, gases, and organic cells and tissue. The type of molecules that bond together and the type of molecular bonds that bind them determine the characteristics of matter. Finally, matter has mass.

Mass is a measure of how much matter there is in an object. The common unit of measure for mass is the pound or the kilogram (one kilogram = 2.2046 pounds). Mass needs a force to start it moving; and when the applied force is removed, it tends to keep moving in the same direction at the same speed. The moving mass has momentum.

Momentum, or inertia, is the natural phenomenon that tends to keep a stationary object at rest and keeps a moving object moving in the same direction at the same velocity. A baseball pitch has momentum. The thrown baseball needs no other force to keep moving other than the thrower's arm. The ball moves because the pitcher applied a force to accelerate it from a speed of zero to ninety miles an hour. It keeps moving because of the natural phenomenon of momentum. It carries the energy of momentum, and it carries that energy of momentum until the energy is transferred to the catcher's mitt, where it decelerates because a force is applied by the catcher's hand.

The earth has momentum. The only thing keeping our earth spinning around the sun is gravity. Electrons have momentum. The only thing keeping them spinning around the nucleus is the force of electrical attraction. *Momentum = mass × acceleration*, where acceleration is the change in velocity used to get an object moving, to get it moving faster, or to stop it.

Velocity is the speed of an object relative to another object. *Velocity = feet/ second.*

Acceleration is the change in velocity per unit of time. *Acceleration = (feet/ second)/sec* = feet/second^2.

Force is an action capable of accelerating an object, so *Force = mass × acceleration = pounds-feet/second^2 (or kilograms-meters/second^2).*

We may tend to think of force in terms of the weight of an object (pounds or kilograms), but in reality, force is more than just weight. Your body is drawn down on a weight scale by the force of gravity. The true units of force are pounds-feet/second^2 or kilogram-meters/second^2.

Mass is measured as the force required to accelerate an object divided by the acceleration produced by that force. So *Mass = Force/Acceleration.* In English units, the unit of mass is the *Slug* (pounds-feet/second^2)/(feet/ second^2), commonly called *pounds (or kilograms)*. Mass is the measure of the amount of matter present.

Energy

Energy is the capacity to do something—the capacity to do work. It may exist in different forms, such as human energy (pushing a wheelbarrow), chemical energy (the combustion engine), thermal energy (home heater), nuclear energy (commercial power plants), and electrical energy (electron flow and electromagnetic energy).

We often confuse energy with work and power. *Work* is the transfer of energy from one source to another, such as using a force to accelerate a mass. *Power* is the rate at which work is done.

Energy can be found in different forms, but all forms of energy may be put into two categories: kinetic energy and potential energy. *Kinetic energy* is energy in motion—electromagnetic waves, atoms, molecules, electron flow (electricity), heat transfer, sound, and motion energy. *Potential energy* is stored energy—gravitational energy; mechanical energy, such as stored or compressed springs; chemical energy stored in the bonds of atoms; and nuclear energy: the energy of fission (splitting nuclei) and fusion (combining nuclei).

My generation of students learned about matter and energy in high school science. Some of us may have learned about them in junior high, or even earlier. From my high school science class, I remember two important facts: 1) Matter cannot be created or destroyed, but only changes form, and 2) Energy cannot be created or destroyed, but only changes form. Many of us have carried these assumptions throughout most of our adult lives.

Then along came the concept of mass energy, which declared that energy and matter are the same and that energy and matter are related by the simple equation $E = MC^2$. In this equation, C equals the speed of light, 300,000 kilometers per second (186,000 miles per second); M equals the mass in kilograms; and E is the energy (300,000 Kg meter^2/second^2). So, what does Kg meter^2/second^2 mean?

Well, it means a mass of one kilogram (2.204 pounds) accelerated at one meter per second squared, moved over a distance of one meter. More simply, it means *energy = force × distance moved.*

The basic unit of energy is the *joule*. It is named after the famous English physicist James Prescott Joule. One joule is the energy expended by a force of one newton moving an object one meter. You may have never heard of James Prescott Joule, but you probably heard of Isaac Newton. A *newton* is the measure of force required to give one kilogram (2.204 pounds) an acceleration of one meter (39 inches) per second. One newton = 1 kilogram meter/second squared. It is commonly called one kilogram.

One joule is the energy required to lift a small apple one meter, and the energy released when the same apple falls to the ground. The earth's gravity exerts an acceleration of 32 feet/second^2 on any falling object, or 9.8 meters/

sec². The energy of one small apple falling one meter is about 1/10 Kg × 9.8 M/sec² × 1 meter ≈ 1 Kg meter²/sec².

Typical energy equivalents may surprise you.

One joule = the force of 1 small apple (about 1/10 Kg or about ¼ pound) falling one meter
One watt second = 1 joule
One calorie = 4 joules
One square foot of sunlight second = 12 joules
One horsepower second = 745 joules
One kilowatt hour = 3.6 million joules
One kilogram (2.2 pounds) of coal = 30 million joules
One gallon gasoline = 120 million joules
One ton TNT = 4 billion joules
One Hiroshima atomic bomb = 15,000 tons TNT
One Bikini Atoll hydrogen bomb = 1,000 Hiroshima atomic bombs

Then there are fireworks. The strength of homebound fireworks varies with the size of the rocket and the aerial displays. I learned all about this when we had a fireworks display in my backyard that drew the attention of the police. Apparently we purchased commercial-grade fireworks. They were spectacular. It was great, until some neighbors called the police. What a bunch of wimps.

Electromagnetic Waves

The *electromagnetic wave* is the God-given miracle of nature that *transmits energy* through space. These waves are generated in various ways. For example, they are generated by varying charges flowing into conductors, such as antennas. They are generated whenever an atom loses energy. They are generated at various frequencies by the sun. And because they are self-sustaining waves (with separate electrical and magnetic fields at right angles to each other), they are self-propagating. They travel forever. Only the strength is lost as they spread out through space. It's a miracle.

There are lots and lots of types of electromagnetic waves. But only a very few electromagnetic waves are visible. Light is visible electromagnetic radiation. Other magnetic radiation produces gamma rays, microwaves, X-rays, and radio waves. All electromagnetic waves have characteristic wavelengths and frequencies. Wavelength is the length of each wave—just like ocean waves, the horizontal distance from top of wave to top of wave. Frequency is the number of times the wave passes a single point in a unit of time.

Conventional practice classifies electromagnetic waves according to frequency in cycles per second and according to wavelength in meters per cycle. The velocity is equal to frequency times wavelength (cycles per second times meters per cycle). Since electromagnetic waves travel at the speed of light, C (300,000 meters/second or 186,000 miles/second), frequency f and wavelength λ are related by the equation $V = f\lambda$. More simply, *wavelength = frequency x the speed of light*, or λ = speed of light/f.

ORDER OF MAGNITUDE ELECTROMAGNETIC WAVES		
Frequency Cycles/Second	Wave Type	Wavelength Meters
60	Commercial Electricity	5000
1,000,000	AM Radio	0.3
100,000,000	TV & FM Radio	0.003
10,000,000,000	Microwaves	0.03/1000
1,000,000,000,000	Infrared Light	0.3/1,000,000
1,000,000,000,000,000	Visible Light	0.3/1,000,000,000
10,000,000,000,000,000	Ultraviolet Rays	3/1,000,000,000
1,000,000,000,000,000,000	X-Rays	0.3/1,000,000,000,000
900,000,000,000,000,000,000	Gamma Rays	0.33/1,000,000,000,000,000

Space is full of fluctuating electromagnetic waves of all possible wavelengths filling it with vast amounts of energy. The *energy associated with electromagnetic waves is fh*, where f is the frequency and h is *Plank's constant* (6.62606896 × 10^{-34} joules). Plank's constant is a proportionality constant that relates the energy E of a *photon* (a bundle of energy, a *bundle of electromagnetic waves*) to the frequency—$E = hf$.

We have learned to use electromagnetic waves for our own benefit. For example, we have learned to resonate (echo) and amplify radio waves into audible sounds. We have learned how to use microwaves for cooking, TV waves for entertainment, and X-rays for medical purposes. The electromagnetic wave is so profound that it encompasses nearly every aspect of our lives.

Electrical Energy

Electricity is work accomplished by the flow of electrons (electrically charged particles), measured in amperes. One *ampere* is the flow of about 6 billion billion electrons in one second. But what makes these electrons flow? What makes them move from atom to atom? It is caused by a force, an *electromagnetic force* (EMF) commonly called *voltage*. Just like water in a pipe, voltage is a pressure. Voltage can be created in several ways, including electromagnetic fields and chemical action.

An electromagnetic force, EMF (*voltage*), may be produced in three ways: moving a conductor across a magnetic field, moving a magnetic field across a conductor, and changing the strength of a magnetic field. That's a miracle. Regarding chemical action, certain combinations of chemicals such as zinc and carbon produce the EMF used in batteries. Certain chemicals in the brain produce EMF used as brain waves. That's a miracle.

Electric charge: The charge of an electron = -1. The charge of a proton = +1. Unlike particles attract, and like particles repel.

Elementary charge: The elementary charge is the charge of one electron = -1.6×10^{-19} coulomb.

One *coulomb* is the electric charge transported by a current of 1 ampere in one second = 6.24×10^{18} electrons.

A *magnetic field* is produced around a conductor when electricity passes through the conductor, like a solenoid (magnetic switch coiled with wire).

An *electric field* is produced when a conductor is passed through a magnetic field, like in a motor.

An *electromagnetic field* is a combination of an electric field and a magnetic field. The changing magnetic field creates an electric field. The changing electric field creates a magnetic field.

An *electromagnetic force or EMF (voltage)* is the potential energy of an electromagnetic field. It can be as large as hundreds of megawatts (10^6) for commercial power generation to milliwatts in the human brain. *EMF is the force that causes electric current to flow.* Amperes cannot be created. Only EMF (voltage) can be created.

Electricity is the presence and flow of electric charge, the natural tendency for electrons to flow from atoms with excess electrons to atoms that need electrons, and in doing so, to accomplish work—to light a lamp, to heat a building, to turn a motor, and so on.

Watts is a unit of power, the rate of doing work. It measures the rate of energy used for production. The smallest measure of energy is the *electron volt*, or the amount of kinetic energy gained by a single electron when it accelerates through an electrostatic potential of one volt. One electron volt = 1.602×10^{-19} joules.

Amperes is the flow of electrons measured as the number of coulombs passing a given point in one second. One ampere = 1 coulomb/second.

Next comes *electrical resistance*. Electrical resistance is the resistance to passage of electrons through electrical wire or other materials through which electricity flows. Resistance is measured in ohms. Resistance generates heat.

Heat causes fire. Electricians size electrical wire large enough to limit the heat generated at the design flow of amperes.

Amperes, voltage, resistance, and power are related as specified in *Ohms Laws*.

Current = I = E/R (amps)
Voltage = E = IR (volts)
Resistance = R = E/I (ohms)
Power = P = EI (watts)

Although the phenomenon of electricity was known to the ancients, it has been understood only the past couple of centuries. Most of what we know and use today was developed in the early twentieth century. What we have not yet done, however, is to learn about, understand, and utilize God's private domain, brain waves.

The Relationship Between Matter and Energy

Albert Einstein related matter and energy in his famous equation $E = MC^2$, where M = mass at rest (in kilograms or pounds), C = the speed of light (300,000 kilometers/second or 186,000 miles/second), and E = energy (joules, kgm^2/sec^2, or pound-mile^2/sec^2). The implications of this equation are enormous.

Nuclear Energy

A few large-nucleus elements, such as uranium and plutonium, have unstable nuclei that naturally decay into smaller nucleus elements. The properties of these elements manifest themselves in the phenomena of nuclear decay, nuclear fission, and nuclear fusion.

Nuclear decay is associated with radioactivity. In the process, an unstable nucleus loses energy by emitting radiation in the form of particles and electromagnetic radiation. The loss of energy results in an atom of one type, called the parent, transforming into a different atom, called the daughter. An example of the use of this is carbon-14 dating, in which carbon-14 slowly transforms into nitrogen 14. The types of decay include alpha emission (two protons and two neutrons) and beta emission (electrons) and gamma emission (electromagnetic radiation). Natural decay times may vary from a few minutes to billions of years, depending on the parent material. Radioactivity also results in the reduction of at-rest mass, which is converted to energy as in the formula $E = MC^2$. Loss of mass is a huge energy producer.

Uranuim-235 is the most common energy producer. Natural uranium consists of only about 0.7 percent U-235. The other 99.3 percent is *U-238*. *Enriched uranium* is uranium in which the percentage of U-235 has been increased. Low-enriched uranium (reactor grade) is 3 to 4 percent U-235, but no more than 20 percent. Highly enriched uranium has greater than 20 percent U-235. Weapons-grade uranium usually contains more than 85 percent U-235.

Uranium is normally enriched by gas centrifuge. First, gaseous uranium hexafluoride (UF6) is chemically manufactured from natural uranium. Next, the gas is run through centrifuges in series. Since U-235 is about 1 percent lighter than U-238, U-235 moves to the inside and U-238 moves to the outside of the rotating elements. The lighter material moves to the next centrifuge, while the heaver material is recycled. Since the centrifuges are in series, each stage produces slightly more concentrated U-235.

For weapons grade, critical mass is about 110 pounds, or a solid sphere about seven inches in diameter. When two masses totaling 110 pounds are brought together in a container lined with a good neutron reflector, a violent massive explosion occurs.

Nuclear fission is the splitting up of the large nuclei into two smaller nuclei. The resulting split produces electromagnetic radiation plus a few free neutrons. With the proper critical mass and under controlled conditions, some of these free neutrons impact other nuclei in a controlled chain reaction. Controlled reactions are used to generate commercial electric power. During the controlled reaction, a great amount of energy is released in the form of heat—dynamic energy from the collisions of neutrons with other atoms. Energy is released principally as kinetic energy from neutrons colliding with other atoms at 7 percent the speed of light, as electromagnetic radiation in the form of gamma rays, and from the fission fragments according to the formula $E = MC^2$.

Power reactors convert the kinetic energy of fission products into heat, which is used to heat water into steam, which then drives a generator. On a weight basis, the available power from nuclear fission is millions of times the power of petroleum fuels. The main downside to nuclear energy is that the waste matter must be handled in a proper manner to protect from exposure to radiation. It is for this reason that the use of nuclear energy is politically sensitive. But nuclear energy is by far the greatest source of energy now available to us.

Nuclear fusion is when like charged particles combine. In nuclear fusion, two protons from different atoms are brought close enough together for their mutual electrical repulsion to be overcome. Examples are two hydrogen atoms or two deuterium (one proton and one neutron) atoms combining to form one helium atom plus one free neutron plus lots and lots of energy. Nuclear fusion is known as the *power of the stars*. Nuclear fusion releases an amount of energy far greater than nuclear fission, but requires very high temperatures to occur, over 200,000,000 degrees Fahrenheit. The hydrogen bomb attains such high temperatures through the detonation of an atomic bomb.

Nuclear weapons result in an uncontrolled reaction and a violent massive explosion accompanied by the presence of dangerous radioactive material. A modern single atomic warhead weighing less than five hundred pounds now has the capacity of over thirty Hiroshima bombs. God has now given mankind the power to completely destroy the entire human race. The construction of these bombs is within the capabilities of many bright people. Nuclear fuel, on the other hand, is at present difficult to obtain. We must all hope and pray that uranium enrichment and the availability of enriched uranium will always be denied to terrorists, warriors, and the criminally insane.

Remarkably, in both controlled and uncontrolled nuclear reactions, only a small amount of mass of fissionable atoms is converted to energy.

Space-Time

Einstein's Theory of Relativity states that time is relative to the speed of the observer. The faster you go, the slower time moves. Everything slows down—clocks, watches, bodily functions.

Don't believe it? Imagine yourself traveling parallel to an electromagnetic wave. Time stops. Imagine you are on the moon watching the World Series on TV. The picture is being sent to you by electromagnetic waves. Imagine somebody hits a home run and you watch the ball sailing out of the stadium. Now imagine you are traveling parallel to the TV wave. Both you and the wave are traveling at the speed of light. Time stops. Since both you and the radio wave travel at the same speed, you always view the same wave location, so time stops.

The Theory of Relativity is just that, a theory, based on assumptions. The special Theory of Relativity makes two assumptions: 1) The laws of physics are the same everywhere in the universe, and 2) The speed of light is always 186,000 miles per second everywhere.

Using these assumptions, it soon becomes obvious that time must slow down as a body speeds up, and time stops at the speed of light. This has to happen if the two basic assumptions are correct. The truth of the first assumption is intuitive: the laws of physics are the same everywhere in the universe. The second assumption, however, is counterintuitive. The speed of light is always the same, no matter how fast the traveler is moving. The speed of light is not added to the speed of the traveler; rather, it is always 186,000 miles per second.

Motion is relative. Einstein likens it to a train and two observers. You are riding on the train. Your friend is watching the train pass by. To your friend, the train is moving; but to you, the train station is moving. You drop a stone from the train. To you, the stone falls straight down; but to your friend, the stone follows a parabola. Motion is relative to the observer.

Time is relative. Both you as the traveler and your friend on the ground see the ball start to drop and reach the ground at the same time. But the ball traveled farther to the observer on the ground than to you. To do that, the observer on the ground had to observe the ball longer than you because the speed of light is absolute. Since distance traveled equals travel time times speed and since the distance traveled was the same, time had to slow down for you relative to the observer.

Einstein derived by simple algebra an equation to express the time passing for an observer on earth to the time passing for an observer traveling near the speed of light. A simplified form of that equation is $T_{Earth} = T_{Traveler}/(1-V^2/C^2)^{1/2}$, where $T_{Traveler}$ = time to the traveling observer, T_{Earth} is time to the observer on the earth, V is the velocity of the traveler, and C is the speed of light. As you can see the time traveled from earth's perspective will always be greater than time traveled from the traveler's perspective because $(1-V^2/C^2)$ is always less than 1. Clocks moving relative to an observer run slower compared to clocks at rest. Note also that as V approaches the speed of light, time to the traveler approaches zero. Time stops at the speed of light.

No mass can travel at the speed of light. Only energy can travel at the speed of light. From what we know now, only electromagnetic wave energy and information can travel at the speed of light. Bear in mind that in our lifetime we have viewed the surface of Mars. That information was transmitted from Mars to Earth by the energy of electromagnetic waves. It is a miracle.

If, at death or at any other time, information such as DNA or mental attitude could be transmitted at the speed of light, that information could reach anywhere in the universe immediately from the perspective of the traveler. If somebody at the other end could read the information and if somebody at the other end had the materials and tools to reconstruct according to whatever information was transmitted, then, technically, life as we know it could be truly eternal.

23 – MONEY

What is money? Where does it come from? How do we get more?

Money is anything accepted as payment for goods and services. It can be actual commodities, such as gold and silver, or it can be representative money, such as currency (banknotes and coins) or demand deposits ("bank money").

"Bank money" does not exist except in the form of various bank records. You may have trouble with that. But it's simple. Your bank records show where your money is. It shows, or is supposed to show, who borrowed it. Whatever isn't borrowed, the federal government borrows every night. Borrowed money is always drawing interest. The bank gets the interest. The bank is supposed to pay you some of the interest. What you don't get, the bank keeps.

Money supply is the total of a country's currency plus bank deposits. Today's money is "fiat money"; it derives its value solely by being declared legal tender by the government. There are no commodities to back up the value of *fiat* money. That money is basically *IOUs* in that the holder of the money is owed equivalent value by the government. For every one dollar you have, the government owes you an equivalent amount of goods or services.

Today's monetary systems are no longer tied to the value of gold. Today's monetary systems are managed by the U.S. *Federal Reserve System*, called the Fed. The *Fed* is an independent branch of government that is not subject to political manipulation or political control. The Fed is a professional entity. Its duties include: 1) conducting monetary policy, 2) supervising all banks, 3) maintaining stability of the financial system, and 4) providing financial service to other banks.

The Fed consists of a board of governors, a central bank, and twelve regional banks. The *board of governors* sets monetary policy by increasing or decreasing the amount of money available. The *central bank* creates money and acts as the bankers' bank by loaning to and borrowing money from member banks and the federal government via authorized agents. The central bank is granted the exclusive privilege to lend a government its currency. *Twelve regional federal reserve banks* provide services to depository institutions and to the federal government, pay Treasury checks, process electronic payments, and issue, transfer, and redeem U.S. government securities.

Most of us listen with interest to the news every night as commentators speak of the Fed. Very few of us understand what the Fed is, let alone several other related agencies. Some of us don't even care. Well, it's time to find out more and become interested, so keep reading.

In addition to the Fed, there are also purely government agencies under the executive branch, including the U.S. Treasury and the Office of Management and Budget.

The U.S. *Department of the Treasury* prints currency and basically sells it to the central bank at cost. The Fed then distributes the currency to member banks and sells some of it back to the U.S. Treasury in exchange for U.S. Treasury securities. It is the U.S. Treasury that cuts checks to pay government bills and entitlements. The Treasury can borrow money only from the central bank. The U.S. Treasury (U.S. government) borrows money from the central bank by selling U.S. government securities (IOUs) to the central bank in exchange for the money.

The U.S. Treasury also collects money and sells and buys U.S. government debt instruments to the central bank on behalf of the U.S. government. Such securities include U.S. government bonds and short-term and long-term Treasury bills. When the amount of money collected from the public through taxes and borrowed by selling U.S. Treasury securities in exchange for cash is not enough to pay all government bills and entitlements, the Treasury of the United States must raise money by selling more securities to the central bank in exchange for money magically created by the central bank. The amount of money owed by the U.S. Treasury is called the national debt. The U.S. Treasury is the U.S. government.

The *U.S. Office of Management and Budget* formulates federal spending plans, oversees preparation of the federal budget, and evaluates the effectiveness of various federal agency programs, an onerous but important task. And of course, there is also the *U.S. Congress*, which passes the U.S. government *budget* authorizing government expenditures, including defense spending, social security payments, transportation expenditures, economic stimulus expenditures (federal giveaways), and pork barrel expenditures (federal government spending for local projects).

These government agencies are independent from the Fed. It is only the Fed that manages monetary policy.

The Fed manages monetary policy with several goals in mind, including maximum employment, stabilization of prices, and moderation of long-term interest rates. The Fed tries to manage our monetary policy by increasing or decreasing the money supply, the amount of money available. This supposedly works because when the money supply is just right, there is enough money around to provide healthy employment, pay entitlements, and provide for the needs of all citizens without creating unsustainable stability or unacceptable inflation.

In any event, we now rely upon the Fed to provide a stable economic system. It tries to do that primarily by affecting the money supply. The bean counters call the shots by magically increasing or decreasing the money supply. The Fed tries to accomplish that by several means. First, it can increase or decrease the interest rates.

By the Fed *increasing interest rates*, people and businesses will borrow less and spend less. This will stabilize prices but increase unemployment. Savers will benefit from high interest rates.

By the Fed *decreasing interest rates*, people and businesses will borrow more and spend more. This may increase employment but will raise prices. Savers will lose because of low interest rates.

During the economic crisis of 2008 to 2009, our economic system nearly collapsed, primarily because people bought more than they could afford. Jobs were lost, as well as many homes. To stimulate the economy, the Fed lowered interest rates to near zero. When that wasn't enough to stimulate the economy, the Fed moved to *quantitative easing*, creating money.

Money is created by the Fed through the central bank *from nothing*. The U.S. Treasury sells government securities to the central bank in exchange for the created money. No physical money is created, but new money magically appears by simply crediting it to the financial records of the central bank, at little or no interest. The national debt is increased by the amount of U.S. government securities purchased from the U.S. Treasury.

The central bank also distributes money by selling U.S. government securities, T-bills, government-backed bonds, or mortgage-backed securities via the open market. Now the new money is in the economy, but the debt instruments of the U.S. government in the U.S. Treasury have increased. The money is distributed to member banks. Money of the central bank is secured by buying securities from those who take the money.

Member banks loan out this borrowed money, and the U.S. government spends the money in any way authorized by Congress, via laws passed by the House of Representatives and approved by the president. The people who benefit from this money are the people who immediately receive it, for instance, the receivers of stimulus money and tax rebates. Others soon benefit as stimulus recipients spend the money, but everybody loses as inflation sets in due to the devaluing of money.

Money can be withdrawn from the economy by the central bank through selling U.S. government securities back to the Treasury, resulting in less money in the economy and less national debt.

And that's the way it now supposedly works. The bean counters run the whole show to create jobs without any input from supply and demand.

What the policy doesn't recognize is the loss of jobs due to cheaper imports and outsourcing (the practice of performing certain labor in and buying certain products and services from other countries rather than our own). There is inherent danger to the U.S. economy and future welfare of our country from excessive imports and outsourcing. First, we are losing productive manufacturing jobs. Second, we as a nation are losing our ability to manufacture. In this country, in addition to college education, we need more technical training, more labor-intensive jobs, economic incentives to manufacture our own goods, and monetary policies sensitive to promoting entrepreneurship and family-owned businesses and farms. We must again learn to take care of ourselves. If we don't, we will lose our world influence. We will be continually in danger of total economic collapse. And we will be in danger of the threat of a socialist state or communist state in the form of, "From each according to his ability; to each according to his need." The problem lies in the danger of losing our ability to provide according to need.

So, how can we as individuals acquire more money? Well, it's simple. In a socialist system, we can acquire more money by getting somebody to give it to us, or we can work for the government. In a well-managed capitalist system, we can acquire more money by working smarter, harder, and longer; by saving; and by investing.

24 – INVESTMENT

This is another tough chapter. If you are not into investments, you will probably skip it. If, however, you are, or if you have investment potential, read on, because to invest intelligently, you must understand the basics. You may, of course, opt to leave your investments in the hands of others, but you still need a general understanding of what is going on to be able to speak intelligently with your investment partner or your broker when they need to consult with you. Investment may be confusing, but it's not rocket science. You just need to know the professional jargon.

At age nineteen, I lost all my money in the stock market. Fortunately, it was only five hundred dollars; unfortunately, it was all the money I had. I had worked three years in high school to buy a $900 car, a beautiful bright green convertible, the highlight of my life thus far. When I went to college, I stored it in my father's garage, only to find at Thanksgiving that my father had sold it for $500, all of which I invested in the stock market in Webb and Knap for one dollar per share. It soon went off the board. I couldn't sell it at any price. I learned one invaluable lesson: *Don't put all your eggs in one basket.* But at the time, I only had one egg.

Every single person in this world needs income. Those able to work and have jobs generate their own income. Those unable to work, and those out of work, need outside income. Outside income may be generated from family members, from the government, or from personal investments. This chapter is devoted exclusively to investments.

Investment is the use of money for future profit, either as periodic income or as *capital growth* (the growth of personal wealth in the form of money or property). Personal wealth doesn't grow from nothing. It needs help. And personal wealth needs to be protected, because there are plenty of people out there trying to take it away from you.

Personal Property

Personal property is the stuff you buy for necessity, pleasure, and investment, such as jewelry, automobiles, antiques, and so forth. When you buy for investment, *buy something good*. It doesn't have to be great or elegant or expensive; but it has to be good.

Real Estate

Real estate investment is common to all of us who own or plan to eventually own homes. Home purchase is something most of us want, but how many of us actually understand it from the real estate investment point of view? Probably not as many as should.

First of all, real estate investment is highly cash flow dependent. The interesting thing about real estate investment is that it is often highly *leveraged* (supported on borrowed money) through a mortgage. Eventually, that mortgage must be paid off. In the meantime, if the property must be sold, the owner realizes all of the *capital appreciation* (increase in net worth after debts and liabilities are paid). When, on the other hand, the property must be sold at a loss, the owner realizes all of the losses—*capital depreciation*. When an investor goes into negative cash flow for a longer time than is sustainable, the property must be sold. The mortgage company normally does not lose; only the property owner loses. In good times it may be sold for a profit. In bad times it must be sold at a loss. Real estate investment can be risky.

It has often been said there is only one important thing about real estate investment—*location, location, and location*. It is always best to purchase a property with distinctive features in a desirable location to ensure the best chances of being able to sell the property quickly. Of course, there is a lot more to consider, such as avoiding overpayment at the time of purchase, acquiring enough for the down payment, maintaining adequate income to cover all costs, and allowing for economic downturn. Economic downturn is usually not a matter of concern for individual homeowners if they can afford to pay the mortgage, taxes, and maintenance costs through the bad times, which is usually the case except for loss of a job.

The risk of losing a job is just one of the risks we all have to take. When all other conditions have been met, you must be willing to take that risk. Real estate investment is time dependent. When you realize and plan for that, there is no danger in buying a home. Even though it may take a long time to get your money out of real estate investment, it is your home. Just don't buy more than you can afford or need. And remember, you have to heat it, cool it, maintain it, and clean it.

Banks

A *bank* is a government-licensed institution that borrows and lends money. Some banks participate in other activities. There are basically three types of banks: retail banks, business banks, and investment banks.

Traditional banks or *retail banks* offer traditional services, such as servicing investors' checking accounts, borrowing money from investors by accepting funds deposited into passbook accounts at relatively low rates of interest, or issuing term *certificates of deposits* (CDs) at somewhat higher rates of interest. The rate of interest on a CD varies with the length of the term; the longer the term, the higher the interest rate. The bank invests your money into conventional investments, such as installment loans and traditional mortgages. Much of the bank's profits are used for salaries, expenses, and the construction of new bank buildings. In times of low interest rates, this means that most of the bank's profits are used for things other than interest payments to depositors.

Most traditional banks insure your deposits under the Federal Deposit Insurance Corporation. At the time of this writing, the insurance limit is $250,000 per depositor per bank. That protects most small investors.

Historically there has been great fluctuation in the interest rates banks pay for savings accounts and CDs. In my lifetime, I have observed interest rates vary from as high as 14 percent to as low as near zero. In the former, the investor is stealing from the borrower. In the latter, the borrower is stealing from the investor. Either extreme case is usury. Unfortunately, we private citizens have little to say about how much interest we receive on our passbook accounts and our CDs. The Federal Reserve decides that, because it decides how much to charge banks to borrow from it. At the time of this writing, the interest rates on passbook accounts are nearly zero. The bank borrows money from us for nothing and loans it out at great profits.

While those with lots of money may invest in higher-paying investments than passbook accounts and CDs, those trying to save with little money to invest, such as children, young adults, and the unemployed, must try to save money when the banks are paying practically no interest. It's unfair. It is a disgrace.

It is also hard to watch our own hard-earned money disappearing through inflation because the Fed is printing money to pay exorbitant and uncontrollable perceived entitlements. This transfer of wealth is criminal, and there is apparently nobody looking out for us.

Business banks provide services to small and midsize businesses and large business entities, and wealth management services to the rich. *Investment banks* trade in securities (stocks and bonds) by dealing with pension funds, mutual funds, and hedge funds.

Large banks offer all three services: retail, business, and investment banking.

Stocks and Bonds
Stocks and bonds are nonphysical assets that are much easier to sell than real estate. *Stocks* are shares in a company. Stocks represent a fractional percentage of ownership in a company. *Bonds* are loans made to corporations and governments. *Mutual funds* are pools of money from many investors used for the buying of stocks or bonds. *Derivatives* are tradable financial products whose value depends on the value of some other asset or combination of assets. In other words, the value of a derivative is guessed at and often highly leveraged (owned with borrowed money).

All investments carry risk. *Risk* is the uncertainty of an investor's return. *Volatility* is the degree to which an investment varies over time. To reduce overall risk, the investor should allow proper asset allocation and diversification.

Each individual investor should clearly identify his *investment objectives.* Stocks and bonds are purchased for growth, income, or both. *Growth* is also called *capital gains*, the growth or loss in *equity* (assess minus debt). *Income* opportunities include *dividends* (periodic payments for stocks) and from *interest* (periodic payments form bonds and CDs).

Investors must also determine how much *risk* they feel comfortable with. Consider what are your available funds?

What is your time horizon before you need the money? Short term would be one to five years. Medium term would be five to ten years. Long term would be ten years or more. What is your life situation? Are you married? Do you have children? Are you retired? What is your salary and how secure is your job? What is your personal response to risk? Do you or do you not worry easily? What is your asset allocation? What percentage of your investments is in stocks, bonds, cash, real estate, and commodities?

Most important of all remember the vital principle of *diversification, diversification, diversification.* Never put all your eggs into one basket.

Stock Investment Analysis
All stock investors buy and sell, either on their own or through a broker. Buyers should always perform a stock analysis before buying or selling any stock. It is stupid to do otherwise. If you are unqualified or if you are not interested in doing it, a broker can perform this service for you. If you try to do it yourself, you may miss something important or you may not clearly understand what you see.

The financial industry has evolved into a jargon of buzzwords designed to convey some sort of meaning unintelligible to the average person. But these are definitions we must learn as independent investors. This is the language of the financial world. Much of it is complicated. Stay away from misleading definitions. They serve to confuse, mislead, and often fool those who want to understand them. There are, however, several definitions that the average investor must understand.

Stock fundamentals involve *assets* (owned property of value), *earnings* (annual profits), and *debt* (borrowed money). Any stock can be evaluated using these three variables. These variables are used to develop simple parameters to evaluate the *value* of any stock; *assets less debt equal equity.*

Earnings per share is the total profit divided by the number of shares. If at the end of the year, a company made one million dollars profit and there were one million shares of company stock, earnings would be one dollar per share.

Price to earnings (PE) ratio is the price of the stock divided by the earnings per share. If the price of the stock was $10 per share and the earnings was $1 per share, the price to earnings ratio (PE) would be 10 ($10/$1). The PE of 10 means the money invested is producing ten percent profit. The part of that paid directly to you is the *dividend.* If the dividend per share is $0.50, your investment produces a yearly income of 5 percent ($0.50/$10). Hopefully the company uses the rest of the profit to increase its capital worth. Unfortunately, some industries use the rest of the profit for ridiculously high bonuses, corporate jets, and political donations.

Beta is the measure of a company's historic volatility. Beta calculations require lots of data and the ability to perform advanced math. A beta factor of 1.0 indicates the stock fluctuates as the average market. Stocks with a beta of less than 1.0 are less volatile. Stocks with a beta of more than 1.0 are more volatile. A beta of 1.1 indicates a stock will rise and fall ten percent faster than the average stock. A beta of 0.9 indicates the stock will rise and fall ten percent less than the average stock.

Price to earnings growth (PEG) is calculated by dividing the PE ratio by the estimated percentage earnings growth rate. If the earnings are expected to double, the projected earnings growth rate is 2. If the current PE ratio is 10, then the PEG would be 10/2, or 5. A low PEG predicts higher profit growth and lower risk than a high PEG.

Debt to asset ratio is calculated by dividing the total company debt by the total company equity (total gross value less debt). If the company debt is $500,000 and the total company worth is $1,000,000, the debt to asset ratio is ($1,000,000-$500,000)/$500,000, or 1.0. Debt to asset ratios of greater than 1.0 indicate the company is financed primarily by debt and is therefore more risky. Debt to asset ratios of less than 1.0 indicate the company is financed primarily by equity (ownership value over and above any liabilities) and are therefore less risky.

Price to book (P/B) ratio is calculated by dividing the stock asking price by the *book value* (assets minus debt, or *equity*). If the asking price of a stock is $1 and the book value per share is $0.50, the price to book value is $1.00/$0.50 = 2. The price to book value is an indication of the price of the stock compared to what it is actually worth. A P/B of 1.0 indicates the price is about the same as the book value. A P/B of less than 1.0 indicates the stock sells for less than the company is actually worth. A P/B value of more than 1.0 indicates the stock is being sold for more than it is actually worth. So why would you buy a stock for more than it is actually worth? You would buy it because it returns a good profit and/or is expected to increase in value.

Stock Orders. There are four main types of stock orders: market order, limit order, stop order, and stop-limit order. A *market order* is an order to buy or sell at market price. A *limit order* specifies the maximum price at which to buy or the minimum price at which to sell. A *stop order* is the same as a limit order except that once the stop price is hit, the stock may be sold at the market price, which may be above or below the stop price. A *stop-limit order* specifies you would be willing to buy or sell a stock if it reaches the stop price but sets a limit above or below the stop price. I personally use only the market order, because I am an investor rather than a trader.

Bond Investment Analysis

As with buying stock, the investor should perform a bond analysis before buying bonds. *Bonds* are loans made by the investor to companies or to the government. Most bonds pay a fixed interest rate until they mature. At maturity, the bond is paid back to the investor at the same price for which it was sold. Government bonds are the safest because they are backed by the U.S. government, which can always pay interest and always buy the bonds back, even if it has to create money to do it.

A *debenture* is an unsecured corporate bond.

Par value is the value of the bond when it was first sold. It is the value printed on the security, and it is the value used to calculate interest payments. Most bonds are issued to pay a uniform interest over their lifetime, regardless of market conditions.

Market value is the amount expected from selling the bond on the open market. Since the bond interest rate is fixed, the market value will fluctuate because overall interest rates will vary and investors will seek the highest rate available at the time. *When interest rates go down, the value of existing bonds goes up.* People will pay a premium to get the higher interest rate. *When the interest rates go up, the value of existing bonds go down,* to compete with new products of higher interest rates. Of course, as the bond approaches maturity, the value closes in on the par value, as the bond is about to be paid off.

A *coupon* is a detachable part of a bond with the date and amount of interest to be paid on a certain date. Coupons must be presented in order to receive payment of interest. The *coupon rate* is the rate of interest the bond pays. Sometimes bonds are sold with the coupons clipped, called *zero coupons*, or bonds that do not pay interest but are initially sold at a discount. In such cases, the bond will sell at a certain discount depending on the maturity date.

Callability is a feature that gives the issuer the right to pay off the bond prematurely. Corporate and government bonds are classified as callable or noncallable at the time of issue.

So, how do you evaluate bonds? Well, why do you buy them? If you buy them for annual income, leave them alone. If you buy them for growth, buy when market interest rates are at their highest and sell when market interest rates are at their lowest. *If you buy at low interest rates, always buy short-term bonds.* If you buy at high interest rates, you may choose to buy long-term bonds because their value will increase when market interest rates fall or until they are called.

Mutual Funds

Mutual funds are pools of money through which investors invest in various sets of stocks and bonds. *Mutual fund types* may take several forms: *active* (actively managed, with lots of buying and selling by the mutual fund), *passive* (index funds, a group of investments that mimic the overall market), *load* (fees are charged to buy), *no-load* (no fees are charged to buy), *open end* (issue as many shares as needed), or *closed end* (fixed number of shares in the pool). They may also be classified by type of investing, such as stock funds, bond funds, or balanced funds (a mix of stocks and bonds).

Stock funds have different characteristics from bond funds. Stock funds may be grouped by total market value of the company's stock (market capitalization): mega cap (over $100 billion), large cap ($10 to $100 billion), medium cap ($2 to $10 billion), small cap ($100 million to $2 billion), or micro cap (less than $100 million). This gives you an idea as to what percentage of the company you own as an investor—not very much as an individual investor, but maybe quite a lot if you are a mutual fund or an *investment bank* (a bank that invests in the market).

Stock funds may also be grouped according to investment style: *growth stock* funds (at least 15 percent return on equity), *value stock* funds (high dividend yield, low PE, low PEG, low P/B), *income* funds (primary goal is income), *emerging markets* funds, and so forth. Most often, stock funds are grouped by sector: energy, financial, health care, nontaxable, foreign stocks, and so on.

There are also *real estate investment trusts (REITs)*. REITs are companies that specialize in real estate and real estate-related industries that generate income. On the upside, REITs are required to distribute 90 percent of their taxable income but act as growth stocks. On the downside, they are risky in that the real estate market may tumble.

Then there is the *hedge fund,* with its aggressive and uncontrolled hungry lion, the hedge fund manager. By name, you would think a hedge fund seeks to offset potential losses by hedging their investments by short selling (selling in a down market to limit their losses). In reality, however, managers are enticed to take risks by giving them 20 to 30 percent bonuses as performance fees without providing any mechanism for them to share in the losses. Unfortunately in the past, the lack of transparency gave rise to abuse and outright fraud.

Bond funds are classified by term: short-term (up to three years), intermediate-term (three to ten years), or long-term (over ten years).

Bond funds are also classified by issuer: U.S. government bonds (Treasury bills called *T-bills* [one month to one year], *Treasury notes* [two to ten years], and *Treasury bonds* [ten to thirty years]); *municipal bonds,* called munis, issued by state and local governments, which have no federal, state, or local tax; *corporate bonds* (issued by corporations); and *junk bonds* (high-yield corporate bonds with substantial risk).

Bonds are assigned *credit ratings* by three major credit-rating agencies: Standard and Poor's (S&P), Moody's, and Fitch. Favorable category ranges include: prime (AAA), high grade (AA- to AA+), and medium grade (BBB- to A+). Everything else is rated non-investment grade, highly speculative, risky, and default. In the past, the rating firms were paid and financed by the very industries and governmental entities that they were rating. Such a practice was a direct conflict of interest.

Options

Options are contracts between a buyer and a seller for the right to buy or sell a particular asset at a specific price. For the buyer, the option is optional. *For the seller, the option is an obligation if and when exercised by the buyer.* All options have built-in time limits.

Typical options include *commodities* (real goods, such as corn and wheat). A speculator promises to buy wheat from a farmer for the present-day price, regardless of any future value. If, in the future, the price of wheat goes up, the speculator makes money and the farmer loses money. If, in the future, the price of wheat goes down, the speculator loses money and the farmer makes money.

There are two common types of stock market options: *puts* (downside markets) and *calls* (upside markets.). The price at which the options may be exercised is called the *strike price*. Strike price is also called the exercise price.

Puts are options that give the *buyer of the put (stock owner)* the option to *limit his potential loss*. Puts are entered into by the buyer (stock owner) by paying a fee to a seller (speculator) for the *seller's obligation to buy the stock at or below the strike price* when the option is exercised by the buyer. Puts limit the buyer's (stock owner's) potential loss.

A *covered put* is one where the buyer owns the stock. A *naked put (short selling)* is where the *buyer does not own the stock*. Naked puts were a major cause of the 2008-2009 economic collapse. Naked puts were declared illegal by the SEC in September 2008.

Puts are basically short selling, as opposed to long selling. *Long selling* is the conventional practice of profit from an increase in the price of an asset. You buy a stock; when the price goes up, you sell the stock for a profit.

Short selling is a strategy of *profiting from the declining value of assets*. In selling short, an investor (speculator) borrows the stock from a third party (usually a broker) for a fee and promises to return the stock at the market value, which may be higher or lower than the borrowing price. The speculator then immediately sells the stock and pockets the money.

At a later date, the speculator repurchases the asset at the market value and returns it to the lender at the then market price. If the price of the stock has fallen, the speculator makes the difference between the original trading price and the returning price. If the price goes up, the speculator loses the difference between the returning price and the initial trading price. Short selling is very dangerous in that hedge funds using computerized trading take huge risks and screw over the individual investor. The individual investor should *avoid short selling*.

Calls are options that give the *buyer (speculator)* the option to buy a stock from the *seller (stock owner)* at an agreed-to strike price if the price of the stock goes up to more than the strike price. If the stock goes above the strike price, the buyer has the option, but not the obligation, to call for the seller to sell the stock to him at the strike price, regardless of the market price.

Calls give the seller (stock owner) the fee and give the buyer (speculator) a chance to make money on a rising stock price without ever owning the stock. The seller's profit is the difference between the high market price and the strike price. On the other hand, if the stock goes down, the buyer merely loses his fee to the seller and the seller retains the stock. When the market price of a stock exceeds the strike price, the call is referred to as *in the money*, because the options may be exercised as a profit for the buyer.

A *covered call* is one where the seller owns the stock. A *naked call* is one where the seller does not own the stock.

Stock owners buy puts (options to limit losses in a falling market) *and sell calls* (commitment to sell at less than the market value in a rising market in exchange for a fee). *Gamblers sell puts* (commitment to buy stock in a falling market in exchange for a fee) *and buy calls* (options to buy stock in a rising market at less than the market value). It's called gambling, but it's much more complicated than at casinos.

Options trading is particularly dangerous for the amateur investor and best left alone. If, however, you want to hedge your bets, you may want to place buy or sell limits with your broker. You may direct computerized buying if the asset falls to a certain price. And you may direct computerized selling if an asset rises to a certain price.

What's Best to Do?

The first thing to do is ask yourself, *"Am I an investor or a trader?"* Do you invest for growth and income, or do you trade for growth and income? If you are a trader, you are nothing other than a drag on society. Go get a real job.

If you are an investor, you have two basic options—do your own investing or use a broker. If you do it yourself, get ready to devote a lot of time to study and research. If you use a broker, you still need to devote some time to study so you can understand and approve of what your broker is doing, While I am no expert, I have devoted enough time to study to derive my own philosophy for investing—*invest for value.*

The greatest stumbling block to investing for value is not having accurate information. Somebody needs to rate the accuracy of investment information; other that that, investing can be simple, easy, fun, interesting, and profitable— but you must be willing to occasionally take a loss. Well-educated investors will do just fine with most of their investments. If you are not a well-educated investor, get a good broker who has your best interests at heart.

25 – TRUTH

The nature of truth is untruth. Truth depends not only on facts, but on the assumptions upon which that truth is based. There is, for example, much difference between scientific truth and biblical truth. Scientific truth is fact-based. Biblical truth is faith-based.

Many of us think of truth as something factual. But truth can refer to things other than factual. It can refer to things perceived, or it can refer to things generally believed, such as religious truth, or it can refer to numerous other definitions developed by the great and not-so-great philosophers of time.

There are objective truths, such as the laws of nature. There are subjective truths, which change with circumstances. Then there are half-truths. History is a perfect example of half-truths. History is written by those who write the history books, mostly academics and biased journalists. Scientists try to do better. Pure science attempts to contain the optimal truth attainable in a given historical period. But sometimes that is difficult to qualify. Different cultures emphasize different aspects of truth. TV and movies heavily influence our perception of truth. Some mystics say that truth can never be revealed by minds thinking; it can be revealed only by meditation. Philosophers are more pragmatic. The job of philosophers is to think through things, determine objective truths, and help the rest of us to understand.

Truth in logic requires truth in all worlds. Truth in mathematics requires statements that are provable in a formal manner. Truth in science requires proof confirmed by peers.

Biblical truth states that truth is not *something*; it is *somebody*, whose name is Jesus Christ, "the way, the truth, and the life."

"Perception is truth." Marketing managers and advertising personnel play that angle all the time.

There is the truth. And then there is to tell the truth. Some lawyers make a living from hiding the truth to protect their clients' interests. Businessmen make a living by telling half-truths, such as advertising only what they want you to hear. There are even academic courses on the art of successful lying, or to be politically correct, selective redirection.

When is it permissible to conceal the truth? Do we tell a loved one when they have terminal cancer? Do we reveal to a loved one our indiscretions? After agonizing over many years, I have concluded it is best to *always tell the truth* unless you are sure the loved one can just not handle the truth. *Truth instills trust and settles the soul.*

26 – LOVE

Are you in love? Have you ever been in love? Why do you think you fell in love?

Love usually starts with interpersonal attraction. It is the attraction between two people that leads to friendships and interpersonal relationships. You may have many interpersonal relationships, but only a few lead to romantic love. Falling in love is not an act of will or a conscious choice. We cannot make it happen. We cannot help who we fall in love with.

Initial romantic love emotions are usually based on physical attractiveness. Initial romantic relationships may be infatuation (irrational temporary passion), a crush (short-lived love), or rapture (great happiness over something or someone).

Interpersonal relationships are best nurtured by propinquity (the more we see, the more we like), similarity (birds of a feather flock together), physical appearance (long relationships are usually formed between people who are equally physically attractive), education, religion, heritage, and interests. Inequity in relationships leads to dissolution of those relationships.

Looking back over my life, I find these elements were present in each of my romantic relationships: my first love, my high school sweetheart, and finally the love of my life, my wife Pam. I liked each of them. I thought I loved each of them. So why, in the first two cases, did the love relationship end?

My first love dumped me after two months for the boy across the street, an aggressive young man who ended up marrying her. I concluded she never loved me and probably never even liked me much. But I loved her.

My high school sweetheart and I drifted apart when I went to college. While I studied in engineering school, she dated several other men, acts that brought me great personal grief. I concluded she liked me but never really loved me. I was just a boyfriend. But I loved her.

The relationship with my wife Pam was different. Pam was very attractive, so attractive that I thought she would never give me a second look. But after knowing each other for a year, she did. Our relationship was a natural fit because we had common backgrounds and common features, except that she was, and still is, much better looking than me and a good deal smarter. She was a very loving and faithful person. She put me on a pedestal. She honored me. She made me happy. She was faithful. I concluded she both liked me and loved me for the most part—well, most of the time.

But there were times in our lives when love seemed to waver. Maybe it was because I sometimes failed to treat her in a loving manner, like the times I was too preoccupied with myself and other things, such as work. Maybe it was because I didn't know how to express my love for her in the manner that she needed. But I always loved her, both in good times and bad. Even so, my inability to demonstrate my love to her in the way she wanted me to caused us great difficulty. My inability to express my love to Pam is the greatest disappointment in my life. I assumed liking her was enough. Never assume another's love. Ask.

Now, looking back, I see that my perception of *like* and *love* was inaccurate and incomplete. *To like is to enjoy something,* such as to like a candy bar or to enjoy being with another person. *To love is not so simple.* Love generates deep emotions, which can take several forms. Various forms and meanings of the word *love* reach back to the ancient Greek language:

Agape is the pure ideal love, love of the soul.

Eros is passionate love, with sexual desire.

Philia is virtuous love, such as loyalty to family, friends, and community.

Storge is natural love, such as is felt by a parent for its offspring.

Xenia is hospitality, such as forms between a host and his guest.

Agape love is universal. In Christianity it stands for God's love for humanity and for God's directions to us. As the Apostle Paul reminds us, "There is little we can know about God now. But after searching for and subsequently discarding all of our conclusions, there are three things that remain—faith, hope and love—and the greatest of these is love."

Eros is sexual love, or lust. Eros love is of particular interest to most all people. After all, everybody's interested in sex. For the young, sexual love is supposed to be off-limits. But there are various stages of eros love that even the young can enjoy. These include intermediate stages of sexual attraction, such as liking, affection, infatuation, and the memorable crush. After those, and only when we are mature enough to deal with it, come passion, marriage, and children. Unfortunately today, over one third of all births in the United States are to unwed mothers. Sexual love is fun, but it is also serious business. It is God's way of ensuring continuation of the human race.

Philia is a continuous and intense attraction and loyalty to family, friends, and community, as opposed to kindness. Most of us will support and defend our family with unyielding and unrelenting support. The same may be said to a lesser extent about our friends and community. We offer general support to our friends and community, but not to the extent that we support our family.

Storge is the love of a parent for a child, a grandchild, or other offspring. Storge is one of the strongest forms of love, especially for mothers. Mothers protect their offspring with undying and unrelenting love.

Xenia is the natural desire to comfort our guests.

I believe that long-term intense loving personal relationships, such as found in marriage, involve and demonstrate all five of these types of love: *agape, eros, philia, storge,* and *xenia.* They happen, but they don't just happen. Something inspires them to develop, sometimes suddenly, sometimes naturally, for others over time. For me, the initial trigger is mutual attraction. You cannot develop a loving relationship alone; it must be mutual. Mutual love grows quickly and exponentially. And that mutual love continues to grow until something happens to turn it off. The mechanism that ends loving relationships varies with each of us depending on our mental makeup, our environment, and our maturity. For me, loving relationships end with unfaithfulness and infidelity. Forgiveness may work, but love is never the same once we have experienced unfaithfulness and infidelity. Unfaithfulness and infidelity usually mark the end of a loving relationship, just as mutual attraction marks the beginning of a loving relationship. Be careful with the one you love; *the line between love and hate is thin.*

In our culture, love is sacred. Early in my life, my father pointed out a prostitute to me and told me to stay away from them. That was good advice. My mother told me when dating to stay within my own age group. That was also good advice. In addition, I gave myself some advice: stay within your own general race. That too was good advice, because that too makes life simpler—simpler for you, simpler for your family, and most importantly simpler for your offspring and for future generations.

In our culture, marriage is sacred. Marriage is sacred even for those who get married just because it's time to get married instead of for love. Some of us may do that. But when we know a person long enough, love will happen if we let it happen. We must honor marriage. We may be attracted to others. We may flirt with others. But we must never cross the line of marital trust and faithfulness. Marriage is sacred.

Work and effort are required to maintain a loving relationship—work and effort that never cease. That is just part of living—it is something we just have to do. Some of us know how to nurture loving relationships; some of us need help. Some of the best advice ever published on how to nurture love is found in 1 Corinthians:

Love is patient. Love is kind.
Love is never jealous or envious, never boastful or proud, never haughty or selfish or rude.
Love does not demand its own way.
It is not irritable or touchy.
It does not hold any grudges and will hardly even notice when others do wrong.
It is never glad about injustice, but rejoices whenever truth wins out.
If you love someone, you will be loyal to him, no matter what the cost.
You will always believe in him, always expect the best of him, and always stand your ground in defending him.

1 Corinthians 13:4–6

Those words of the Apostle Paul tell us in no uncertain terms what pure, ideal love expects from us. We must strive always, for our entire lives, to nurture love, even when love generates less desirable emotions, such as possessiveness and jealousy. Possessiveness can be as disruptive to a relationship as infidelity. In the marriage vows, we promise to love, honor, and cherish. We love, honor, and cherish our marriage partner, but we do not own our marriage partner. Even after marriage, it's still a free country.

Marriage is a social union before God and a legal contract between two people, a man and a woman. Legally, marriage gives each spouse control over the other's sexual services, labor, and property; responsibility for debt; visitation rights when incarcerated or hospitalized; control over affairs when the spouse is incapacitated; legal guardianship of children; financial obligations to the children; and relationships between families. These are legal rights of married people. They are not wedding vows.

Wedding vows are different. Wedding vows are the vows each spouse makes to the partner in the presence of God, such as "to love, honor, and cherish." Legally, such vows are meaningless except for the word "yes" when asked the question, "Do you take this person to be your lawfully wedded husband/wife?" It is only after the pastor, the mayor, or other legal officiating officer says, "I now pronounce you husband and wife," that the couple is legally bound to meet the responsibilities of marriage. We may be legally bound to the marriage union. But we are never legally bound to the wedding vows. For the wedding vows, we are bound to God.

True love is not simple. True love takes time and commitment. The art of true love must be learned. And once learned, true love must be exercised to make it work—be it universal love, sexual love, love of family, protection of children, or comfort of guests. Love takes work. Love takes commitment. *Love is the presence of God.*

27 – HAPPINESS

Nothing is more important than happiness. Nothing even is a close second. But what is happiness, and how do we find it?

Believe it or not, happiness has absolutely nothing to do with looks, IQ, education, health, or economic status. Happiness depends upon our perceptions and on the quality of our relationships with other people.

Happiness is a state of mind—a general feeling of well-being, no matter what happens, as opposed to *joy*, which is temporary elation. Happiness is an attitude—an attitude that reflects our feelings at any particular moment. Although our feelings are influenced by memories of the past and anticipation of the future, it is in the present that we find our happiness or unhappiness. I should know, because I spent much of my life regretting the past, worrying about the future, and resenting the present. In that process, I learned a lot about happiness.

First, to be happy, you must develop a positive attitude. Look at the half-full glass rather than the half-empty glass. It is simply impossible to be happy without developing a positive outlook. Why is that so difficult for some of us?

There is a school of thought that believes some people are more prone to depression because the tendency for depression is in our genes. Maybe someday we will find out which genes they are and learn how to modify them for more favorable results. There is another school of thought that believes the tendency for depression is instilled in us between the ages of two and five, because that is when the brain learns the fastest. Others believe depression is a result of how we were treated as older children. Still others, like me, believe depression is caused as a result of loss, disappointment, and defeat.

Regardless of how susceptible we are to depression, there are certain things we can do to alleviate or even eliminate our depression.

About one third of us have serious mental problems in our lifetime. Those of us who do must seek counseling and take proper medications. The brain is a fragile instrument, whose function is dependent upon a proper chemical balance (see "Body, Mind, and Soul"). *Monoamines*, such as *serotonin* and *dopamine* (the brain's pleasure chemical), are major neurotransmitters affecting depression and happiness. The imbalance of critical chemicals required by our neurotransmitters is unforgiving. Each of us must take responsibility for maintaining proper chemical conditions for good mental health.

The rest of us can train ourselves to be happy. That is not always easy, but it can be accomplished with proper direction. The strategies and tactics to overcome depression and find happiness have been taught since the time of the early Greeks, the early Israelites, and the early Christians. The principles haven't really changed much. It is truly amazing how much our ancestors knew.

First and foremost, *maintain a positive attitude*. Drop negative self-perceptions. As straightforward as this sounds, there are times in each of our lives where this is very difficult—such as in times of great loss and in times of severe and repeated defeats. In these times, there is no half-full glass, only an empty glass. In cases like this, it is time to beg, borrow, or steal water. Go find new sources of happiness. Don't push your problems off onto somebody else.

Second, *find your own happiness*. Too many of us look to others to find happiness. We each must find our own happiness. Each of us is responsible for that. Each of us must do that. Show courage facing setbacks and defeats. When necessary, find your happiness elsewhere. Find another friend. Find another church. Find another place to hang out. Plan a trip. Read. Write. Take a night course.

Third, *don't compare yourself with others*. Believe it or not, nobody really cares who you are, what your talents are, or what you have done, except you. Comparing yourself with others leads to envy, and envy leads to depression.

Fourth, *set attainable goals*. Unattainable goals cause depression. Take small steps to find out where your talents lie, what you are good at, and what you enjoy doing. Don't ever sell yourself short. Always believe you can have anything in the world you want, because you can. There are many things you can do to attain your goals, including training, practice, and stick-to-itiveness. If available to you, learn to sail; learn how to tack and jibe. Take a Dale Carnegie course or join Toastmasters. Just remember that even though *there are some things you just can't do*, there is great power and *joy in imagination*.

And fifth, *learn how to control your mind*, regardless of the current situation. This can be difficult, particularly if you don't know how the mind works. Take time to learn; those who don't may experience mental health problems. Each of us must develop our own best coping mechanisms.

Coping mechanisms are the tactics used to battle depression after our strategic goals have been achieved—the tactics used after we have sought counseling, after we are on the proper medications. Like some of you, I have experienced depression. Over a period of many years, I tried many coping mechanisms. Some worked; some didn't. Some worked to an extent, but none worked alone.

Each of us has known loss and disappointment, some of us more than others. My losses and disappointments have been much less than others', so why did I become depressed over little things? It was because of the personal humiliations of repeated loss, disappointment, and failure.

I discovered loss and disappointment at age fifteen. Before then, I had a happy childhood. Up to then, I was basically a happy person. At the beginning of my sophomore year in high school, I was selected to play quarterback for my high school football team. I only weighed a hundred and forty pounds. I couldn't run very fast, but I could throw the football. Our team had been playing football for only about five years. The school had won a few games. As a freshman, I had watched football games from the stands dressed in my band uniform. The players looked awfully big. I wasn't sure I could tackle any of them, but I decided to try. I didn't go out for any particular position; I just went out to see if I could play.

That year before football season, our entire team went to football camp. When we arrived at camp, I was selected to play quarterback. The coaches trained me in every move to make, how to throw a pass, how to block, and how to tackle. Unfortunately, passing practice was limited to simple run-out passes to open receivers. We never practiced passing against defensive backs. I was also trained to turn my back on the defense and fake handoffs before turning to pass. Unfortunately, that was also a terrible mistake.

In my first game, I had six passes intercepted. I went home that night, went directly to bed, and cried. I felt that I had let the team down, I had let my school down, and I had let my hometown down. I vowed never to do that again.

But vowing victory didn't make it happen. It didn't make victory happen that year, or the next year, or the next year. I played high school football for three years. During those three years, I never ever sat on the bench and watched. I played every minute of every game, offense and defense. We repeatedly lost. Out of twenty-three football games, we won only one; we tied one game, and we lost twenty-one. The one game we won was wonderful; we rode all over town blowing car horns, without ever thinking about the other team. There is no instant gratification like victory. The tie was a waste of time. Nobody on either team was happy. I have never thought much about the game we won or the game we tied. Those memories didn't make much of an impression on my mind. It was the losses that affected me emotionally; the repeated losses were devastating.

I have carried those humbling experiences with me my entire life. Those repeated losses became the seat of my depression. If only I had known how to deal with that … but I did not. Medication helps a great deal, but that alone does not erase depressing thoughts of the past. Counseling also helped. Counseling teaches us to view matters from a different perspective. But medication and counseling alone will not totally eliminate depression.

Each of us must find our own tactics to stop those recurring negative thoughts. We must each learn to erect *mental traffic signs,* such as *stop* and *do not enter.* In other words, don't go there. Do not allow depressing thoughts to travel those old roads to depression. Refer those initial negative thoughts that do get through to a lockbox, or better still, a shredder. The only person in the world that negative thoughts hurt is you. Nobody else cares.

I did not learn how to deal with my depression until later in life. Now, finally, I have learned to control my mind to weed out depressing thoughts. After many years of failure to cope with depressing thoughts, I have learned to erect traffic signs in my mind, stop signs and no trespassing signs. I have found that this works for me. Just have those signs pop up whenever the neurons sense depressing thoughts. And when other people don't care enough not to injure you mentally, get away from them, far away. Find new friends, find new interests, and find new activities.

My little story may be of little interest to you. You have your own stories, stories that are yours and nobody else's. Only you have to deal with them. Only you can deal with them. My prayer is that you learn to deal with them effectively. Take time to learn and understand how the mind works. And remember always, *"You can't be happy and unhappy at the same time. So be happy."*

Simplify your life. Put things in proper perspective. Think thoughts of perfection. Remember that your mind has little control over this world, so you worrying about things you can't control won't do much good. Work at the things you can control. Don't dwell on things you can't control.

Imagine that you are attracting everything that comes into your life. Imagine your mind is a magnet. You have about sixty thousand thoughts a day; hold onto the thoughts you really want and let the other thoughts pass by. Meditate or pray daily.

Learn how to manage stress properly. During times of stress, try to relax. There is tremendous peace, joy, and beauty within you. Just accept that, and you will begin to feel it. Turn every thought into a positive thought. *Push the happy button.*

28 – THINKING, GOD, AND PRAYER

Thinking and praying are two different things. Thinking is talking to ourselves. Praying is talking to God.

Thinking

Thinking is the *use of the mind to form thoughts.* The mind then uses those thoughts to form opinions and arrive at conclusions. Thinking is electrochemical activity in which the brain allows us to model and effectively deal with our world. Thinking may be a thought, an image, a sound, an idea, or an emotional feeling. The essence of thinking includes consciousness, imagination, perception, cognition, reason, and reasoning. The types of thought include awareness, creativity, critical thinking, decision making, erroneous thinking, learning and memory, and reasoning.

An independent mind lies within each individual. That mind is ours and ours alone. Nobody else can view it. But anybody can influence it, and thereby influence the way we think. The thinking mind includes both the rational and the irrational. The rational mind is capable of reason and reflection. The irrational mind is emotion, the decision maker.

Early in my professional career, I was lucky enough to be sent to a one-week class in value engineering. Value engineering is a discipline used by designers in the construction industry to reduce the cost of over budget projects by selective redesign without interfering with the proper function of the overall project. There are three separate stages in value engineering. There is the information gathering stage, the creative thinking stage, and the decision stage. During the creative thinking process, no idea is stupid. The dumbest idea may lead to a follow-up idea, and then another follow-up idea, until a really good idea is reached.

Another bit of advice was gleaned from Alfred Armand Montapert's

The Supreme Philosophy of Man: "Maintain a healthy mind." He pointed out that the three steps to maintaining a healthy mind are: 1) control anger and passions of the mind, 2) the conquest of fear, and 3) the elimination of worry.

God

God is universally referred to as the all-powerful, all-knowing creator and overseer of the universe—creator of heaven and earth, the stars of the sky, the day and the night, the fishes of the sea, and the animals of the earth. He is also the creator of the first man and creator of the first woman.

Does God exist? What is God? What does God look like? And can the presence of God be proven? Present-day arguments are now mainly over *intelligent design.* Intelligent design asserts that features of the universe are best explained by an intelligent cause, not an undirected process of natural selection. To me, the matter of intelligent design is a moot point because the theory of evolution is not inconsistent with the creationist view. The bottom line is that everything was made. Everything was made according to the natural laws of nature and the laws of the universe, even though we don't yet understand a lot of things, such as black holes and parallel universes.

I believe God does exist. How else could all of this have been created? The only question is, who is God? What is God?

Religions exist because man needs them. Man needs them for their moral values, for their governing social values, and for peace of mind. People choose, and have chosen in the past, those concepts of God set forth by the specific religions that work best for them. Theologians and philosophers attribute several attributes to God, including omniscience (God knows all and knows how humans will act of free will), omnipotence (all-powerful), omnipresence (always present everywhere), perfect goodness, and divine simplicity.

God has been described as incorporeal (without physical being), a personal being (a living thing), the source of all moral obligation, and the greatest being. More recently God has been called the universal way and the source of all energy and being. No matter which of these definitions you support, there is no proof of God's existence. There is only faith (belief and trust). Faith is not perfect reason, but requires risk. Faith requires spiritual risk without logical proof. To manage spiritual risk, there are several theological approaches:

Theism generally holds that God created and sustains everything. God is omnipotent, beneficent, and interactive with the universe. God is infinite, yet somehow is present in the affairs of the world.

Deism holds that God is wholly translucent (allowing light to pass through but only diffusely, and that objects cannot be distinguished). God exists but does not intervene in the world beyond what was necessary to create it. In

118

this case, God does not answer prayers or cause miracles to occur. God plays dice.

Monotheists hold there is only one God.

Pluralists believe their religion is right but do not deny the partial truth of other religions.

Exclusivists believe they have exclusive access to the truth.

Relativists believe everybody is right.

Pantheism holds that God is the universe and the universe is God.

Atheists believe there is no God.

Agnostics believe no one knows whether or not God exists.

Me personally, I am a Christian. I believe in Jesus Christ. I believe Jesus was God on earth. I believe that Jesus died for our sins. I believe that my sins are forgiven and I will spend eternity in heaven. With all those guys in white robes and red caps running around Rome, how could I believe differently? Furthermore, Christianity is a really good deal.

Many religions hold that God is a being that influences our day-to-day existence. For those religions, there is prayer.

PRAYER

Prayer is talking to God. Prayer is not thinking. We have to understand the difference between praying and thinking. We think logically and emotionally to ourselves. We also pray logically and emotionally, but prayer is talking to God.

When do we pray? Why do we pray? What do we say when we pray? The answers to those questions are probably different for each of us. We can pray anyplace anytime. Some of us pray in church, some pray publicly, some pray alone. Some never pray.

Church services invoke formal prayer, hymns, liturgy, and a world of gratitude or a spontaneous utterance. Most major religions of the world invoke prayer in one form or another in their rituals. To me, formal prayer may occasionally be meaningful, but in general, it is personal prayer that offers the most comfort and positive influence. As Jesus stated in Matthew 6:6, "When you pray, go into your room, close the door and pray to your Father, who is unseen."

Prayer means talking to God in a reverent way. It may be a morning prayer, an evening prayer, or a spontaneous prayer. Sometimes there is an advantage to being in constant communication with God, often through meditation. There is a pronounced difference between thinking and praying. For me, there is a reverent *click* when starting to talk to God. There is a *click* the moment I say, "Dear God." For the evening prayer, I make a practice of praying for four things: praise, thanks, forgiveness, and needs.

After the *click, praise* God. God is great, God is wonderful, God is magnificent, and God is awesome. After praise, pray *thanks*. Thank God for the blessings bestowed upon you and your loved ones. After thanks, pray for *forgiveness*. Forgiveness cleanses the soul and makes us new. After forgiveness, pray for *needs*. Pray first for the needs of your loved ones and then for your own needs.

Sometimes we pray for help, sometimes for comfort. None of us can interpret the ways of God. We can only trust. We pray because we need God. Sometimes we simply need to spend time with God. We do not pray to tell God anything. He already knows. When we pray, we stand by God and look with him toward people and problems. We speak to him as we speak to our most intimate and trusted friends. Ultimately, prayer proves its power by changing us. *Prayer is like taking time to let God recreate us.*

With all the sadness, suffering, and disappointment in this world, do you sometimes wonder whether there is anybody really listening? Is there really a God? If there is a God, does he really care? Why doesn't he answer our prayers? Why do we pray? Does it do any good? What's the point?

The point is that Jesus taught us to pray. Jesus never wondered if God exists. Jesus was God on earth. Jesus was the world's greatest lover. He came to this earth to teach us how to love. Jesus never wondered whether anyone was listening; he never questioned the importance of prayer. Jesus would flee the crowds to spend time with God in spirit. Jesus would get up early, before sunrise, and pray. Prayer served as his refuge, his strength, and his guidance. That doesn't mean that Jesus didn't experience the frustration of unanswered prayer, such as he prayed in Gethsemane.

Yes, there are times when we may ask, "Is there a God?" No, we do not understand the ways of God, but we must trust in God's ways and we must have faith. Just look around you. Look around you at the miracles of life. Just think about the billions of living cells in the human body. Just think about the billions of stars in our Milky Way galaxy. Just think about the billions of galaxies in the universe. Just think about the natural laws of nature. Yes, there is a God. Even Albert Einstein believed in God. Once, when asked for a recommendation for a research paper, Einstein replied, "Find out about prayer."

As Christians, we believe that *God chose to leave within each of us the Holy Spirit*. We talk to him through that Holy Spirit. When we pray, it is the spirit of God praying within us. When you pray to God, always listen for the *click*. Praying is talking to God.

29 – CARE

"Take care."

We all say that at one time or another, usually as an affectionate farewell. But the word *care* means more than that. *Care* can mean to feel affection, to be concerned, to take care of somebody, to like somebody or something, or to worry; to provide social welfare, personal care, medical care, or legal oversight and attention; or to behave prudently or to deal effectively with somebody or something.

Care carries several connotations. First and foremost, we think of *caution* in avoiding harm or danger. Second, we feel *affection and concern*. And third, we think of effectively *providing for needs*.

Care is a respected discipline, particularly in the form of providing for the needs of those unable to care for themselves. Caregiving is sometimes provided at great personal sacrifice; sometimes it is given naturally. Sometimes caregiving is not recognized or appreciated. Sometimes we don't even know we are being cared for. And sometimes we don't even know we are giving care. But when recognized, there is great comfort in caregiving, for both the cared-for and the caregiver.

You don't have to be a formal caregiver to provide care. Each of us care and is cared for every day of our lives. In today's world, *we are trained to depend on others for practically everything.* Unlike frontier days, when everybody took care of themselves, today most of us lack the ability to do much of anything. To care for others, we must first of all be prepared to offer care. We can't do that until we are mentally, financially, and physically equipped to provide care. To do that, we must first care for ourselves.

Take care of yourself first. Then take care of the people who take care of you. Then take care of others in need. And *don't slap the hand that feeds you.*

We may also care about other people and personal relationships. We may feel interest about someone or something. We may care about another person, develop concerns, develop friendships, or love.

Or we may care about things, like the old homestead or our childhood school or church—or about our stamp or coin collection, antiques, money, or investments. We may also care about personal interests, like reading, learning, or philosophy. Some of us may care about winning. Others may care about their job or meeting the next car payment or mortgage payment.

We usually care about things that bring us security, happiness, and joy. And we are all different. We all think differently. We all care about different things. Sometimes a lot of us care. Sometimes only some of us care—like those who care enough to read this book. To those who have read it, I thank you, with hopes it will give you a few ideas to grow with and build upon.

30 – PROGRESS

One thing in life is absolutely certain—change.

That's the way it is. That's the way it's always been—since the beginning of time, since the beginning of man, since Adam and Eve, since the beginning of recorded history. *Change is inevitable.*

The significance of change became evident to me when, after four years out of engineering school, the structural design codes changed. After struggling to learn my professional skills, the demand for those skills suddenly changed from what I had learned to what I had to learn anew.

I had a friend in college who liked making a fool of himself by often saying, "Time marches on." It still irritates me that I can't get that saying out of my mind. I often say it when faced with a problem when I have no idea what to do. But it is true. Time stops for no man, except when traveling at the speed of light.

The longer we live, the faster time seems to travel. Looking back, it seems incredible that the Holocene epoch, the time when humans began to have a significant impact on the earth, began in only 10,000 BC (the end of the last Ice Age). It was about that time that humans began converting from hunters/gatherers to agriculturalists. Their tools were basically made of stone.

The Stone Age generally refers to prehistoric times (before recorded history). Depended upon location on the earth, the Stone Age supposedly ended between 6000 BC and 2500 BC. Then came the Copper Age or primitive metalworking age (5000 to 3000 BC); the Bronze Age or advanced metalworking age (3000 to 1200 BC);, and the Iron Age (1800 to 200 BC), when tools and weapons were made of iron and steel. Other time periods are referred to as historical periods: Ancient History (3500 BC to AD 300), Middle Ages (300 to AD 1400), Early Modern (1400 to AD 1700), and Modern (1700 to present).

The theory of evolution is not inconsistent with religious teachings. We could debate forever over divine creation. The question is, when did Adam and Eve appear?

In human evolution, man is defined as *Homo sapiens* (Latin for wise man or knowing man). There are those of us who believe evidence shows Adam and Eve appeared within the last 12,000 years. It was during that period that man became wise.

Recorded history began in Mesopotamia, which is present-day Iraq, around 3500 BC, in Egypt about 3300 BC, in China 3000 BC, North America 2000 BC, and South America 1800 BC.

Greek mythology refers to the early ages of man as the Golden Age, the Silver Age, and the Bronze Age.

In the Golden Age, peace and harmony prevailed. Humans did not have to work to feed themselves. Man was good and noble. So what happened to the Golden Age? Why did Adam and Eve have to pick and eat the apple from the tree of the knowledge of good and evil?

During the Silver Age, humans spent most of their time in strife; men refused to worship gods. During the Bronze Age, men were hard. War was their purpose and passion. But the early wise man was also smart and creative.

It is incredible that today we can witness the remains of what the early wise men knew and understood. It is amazing to see remains of physical accomplishments of history: the Egyptian pyramids (2600 BC), Peru's Machu Picchu (AD 1400), Greece's Parthenon (450 BC), and Rome's Coliseum (AD 70).

The Middle Ages (300 to 1400) were eventful, but much was lost during the Dark Ages (300 to 900). Unbridled military expansion occurred during the High Middle Ages (1000 to 1450). Wonderful artwork was produced during the European Renaissance (fourteenth and fifteenth centuries).

But the world really began to change at a rapid rate with the Age of Discovery (fifteenth to sixteenth centuries), when explorers roamed the world. New rules of reason were developed during the Age of Enlightenment (eighteenth century). Great technological changes occurred during the Industrial Revolution (eighteenth and nineteenth centuries). Things seemed wonderful until the Machine Age (1900 to 1945). It was the Machine Age that ushered in the Age of Oil (1900 to present), World War I, World War II, Korea, Vietnam, and the Oil Wars of the Middle East. The Atomic Age began in 1945. The Space Age began in 1957. The Information Age began in 1970.

How did mankind survive such changes? The common theme that helped humans survive change was *motivation*. Motivation is an emotion felt in the search for satisfaction and the avoidance of conflict. During all of these time periods, there were the haves and the have-nots, the rich and the poor, the educated and the uneducated, the powerful and the powerless. Those with knowledge, wisdom, and courage led. Those without knowledge tried to survive. It is knowledge that marks the economic and social boundaries of society. *Knowledge is power.* That's the way it is. That's the way it's always been.

Some people have always had knowledge and wisdom. It was less than five thousand years ago that the Egyptians built the pyramids. Some people had the knowledge to build them; others did the work of building in exchange for food, shelter, and beer.

During the twentieth century, a college education pretty much assured a person was going to have a good chance of making it in their professional careers. But in this present Information Age, knowledge is cheap. The worldwide Internet makes knowledge immediately accessible to practically everyone.

It was just three thousand years ago that the Greeks wrote of the moral philosophy we still follow today. Only twenty-five hundred years ago, the Torah was written; and only two thousand years ago, the Bible was written. These documents were written by those with the knowledge and wisdom to do so. The rest of us try to follow their teachings.

It was only 650 years ago that the Gutenberg Bible was published and the printed word was born.

It was only five hundred years ago that Columbus discovered America for the Europeans. That discovery ended the lives through disease and military force of native Americans who had the knowledge and wisdom to have built the likes of the city of Machu Picchu in the mountains of Peru and the Mayan Temple at Tikal in Guatemala.

It was only one hundred years ago that humans discovered and learned how to use electricity, how to magically define and develop the rules of chemistry and handle chemical concoctions used in our society, and how to harness the atom for destruction and for peaceful purposes. All of these disciplines take knowledge—in many cases a lot of knowledge; in some cases knowledge denied because of corporate security, patents, or prohibitive expense.

Through all of these changes, man has had to learn and learn anew skills to cope with society, to secure a job, and to just survive in an unforgiving world. Now, the need to learn and learn anew is even more important than ever. Now there is so much information out there that it is impossible to master it all or even a small portion of it.

But we can still learn and familiarize ourselves with the basics. We can learn how to access the knowledge and information we need to deal with progress. And, short of that, we can learn to do what we are told when baby needs a new pair of shoes.

The days of securing knowledge with a formal college education are changing. In today's Information Age, education has been upended by solid-state electronics and the computer.

Solid-state electronics are electrical circuits built entirely from solid materials in which the electrons are confined entirely within the solid material. Such solid elements are engineered to switch and amplify electrical signals when a small voltage is applied at the right place at the right time. The current flows in two forms, negatively charged electrons and positively charged electron deficiencies called electron holes. These electrons and electron holes are stored in semiconductors, such as silicon highly processed and doped (chemically treated).

Semiconductors are the foundation of the basic tools of solid-state electronics because these semiconductors (most often processed silicon) may be miniaturized and layered with capacitors (that store electrical charges as an electron, or stored as no charge) and transistors (switches that also amplify a signal) that have been miniaturized to the point where they may be less than 1/200 the diameter of a human hair. Millions of capacitors and transistors may be stored on a single chip the size of your fingernail. Along with these are logic circuits with "if" switches (if greater than, go to someplace; and if less than, go to someplace else) and other logic tools, all of which are now packaged in a light plastic housing that fits in the palm of your hand.

Storage locations (charge or no charge) are accessed by a shift register, which is wired as a circuit to access storage units at the right place and at the right time.

To confuse the issue is the jargon of the trade. To understand what is going on, you have to recognize technical names and their meanings, the same as in any other discipline. Such devices include silicon computer chips doped and layered, embedded with, and topped with logic boards, transistors, DRAMs (dynamic random access memory), and other data storage and data processing devices.

We have to decide what we want to become familiar with, what we want to learn, and what we want to master.

There are some things we just can't do because of the limitations of intellect, natural talent, environment, or will. There are some things we just can't do—at a given time. But given time, we can do many things we once thought we couldn't do. A good friend of mine played third trombone to me in high school. That was fifty years ago. Now I have lost my lip, but my friend is a world-class New Orleans Dixieland trombonist. How did he do it? Well, to begin with, he had a little talent. He knew what he wanted to do. He had determination. He found the right environment to progress his talent. I love to hear his Dixieland Band play. They are really great. But to become that good, each of them paid a price.

We can have most everything we want in this world if we are willing to pay the price. But we always must ask, "Is it worth it?" If it is, we keep working at it. If it isn't, we drop it.

In dealing with life, we are constantly dealing with change. Somebody or something is always changing—sometimes for the best, sometimes for the worst—but something is always changing. We hope that change is progress. Religious changes two thousand years ago were certainly progress. The Era of Discovery and the Era of Enlightenment certainly demonstrated progress. Scientific discovery of the nineteenth and twentieth centuries certainly demonstrated progress. We hope and believe today's changes are still progress. We hope and pray the twenty-first century envelops the right kind of progress. We pray and hope the future changes are ones that demand our best and produce the best, rather than just creating busywork.

One thing is clear: many current changes threaten to rob us of our independence. Today, we rely on other people for practically everything. In addition, automation has eliminated many jobs that people need for mental, physical, and financial welfare. We must learn how to deal with progress so that our mental, physical, and financial needs are met. Some people believe that requires a complete change in social patterns. Others believe it demands more education, more sacrifice, more time, and more wisdom than we have. Others simply don't care. But whatever our philosophical beliefs, we will, as always, do whatever we have to do to survive and to ensure the survival of our offspring.

We see creeping up on us the creation of useless, stay-busy jobs. And by that I also mean professional stay-busy jobs created by government and social bureaucracy. Frankly, stay-busy jobs are a waste of money. We don't need them. We would be better off educating people for employment in jobs that provide real products and services. We would be better off keeping what works instead of developing new and cheaper but less reliable ways to do things just because economics demands it. The creation of busy jobs is not progress. True progress comes from improving the services and things that we already have and developing new technologies that are needed to survive. That means finding new approaches to developing new energy sources, learning more about how we think, and becoming wiser people.

True progress should be the way to a happier and more secure life, rather than one filled with stress and insecurity. True progress should be defined and directed by truly wise philosophical people. True progress will never be found by politicians and money-grubbers. True progress is found by philosophers.

I hope that you, in the development of your own personal philosophy, turn to wise people for direction. I hope that you, in your busy life, find time to learn how to learn, how to study, how to work, how to play, and how to rest.

I hope that you, in the living of your life, master the art of making wise choices and the wisdom, courage, and stamina to make those choices work for you and your loved ones.

I hope that you, in the living of your life, learn joy in serving others and learn how to enjoy living. Just remember what Granddaddy said about getting along with others, *"Don't get stuck in the first person singular."* And when you do, *"Take out the word I and put in the word you."* To do that takes practice, courage, and resolve. Remember, *it's not what you say, but the way you say it.*

Somebody once told me, *"It's not the destination, but the journey."* Well, he was only partially right. It is the journey, but it is also the destination. *Know where you are headed,* try to figure out what is best to do, then go as fast as you can and see what happens.

What happens is progress.

31 – CLOSURE

Closure is the end—the end of business, the end of access. Sometimes closure just happens; sometimes we must initiate it. When it just happens, we just have to accept it. We also have to accept it when we initiate it. Accepting closure is usually relatively easy, but it takes resoluteness, a sense of determination, and purposefulness. Deciding to instigate closure is not so easy. Deciding when to instigate closure is tough.

Like the song says, "You have to *know when to fold them.*" Presumably the song refers to stopping your losses. But closure has several other meanings. In psychology, closure refers to the conclusion of a traumatic event in a person's life. In philosophy, it refers to a temporary resting place for ideas and concerns that do not offer final answers.

Both psychological and philosophical closures are brought about by the need for cognitive closure, closure of mental functions and mental processes. Some individuals have a higher need for closure; others have a lower need for closure. A person with a high need for closure prefers order and predictability. A person with low need for closure is more thought-forming and creative.

The degree of closure will, of course, vary with the person and the situation. At one end of the scale is the closed container. The container stays closed until the person wants to open it. At the other end of the scale is death. *Nothing is quite so final as death.*

It is in the middle scale where we most often find ourselves—closure from embarrassment, closure from loss, closure of a project, closure of an effort. All of these cases result in cognitive relief—a well-needed rest of the brain and relief from emotional stress. Closure provides all of these. But equally important, closure marks the beginning of the new: the new love, the new project, the new interest. To begin anew, we must first feel a sense of finality.

It is the sense of finality toward which we direct our efforts to find cognitive relief. That sense of finality comes with decision—a decision to stop, a decision to close. Most times that decision is yours and yours alone. Most times that decision is irreversible. It is a decision that you must live with. *Evaluate it wisely.* Make the decision as directed in Ecclesiastes 3:1, *"There is a right time for everything."* I believe God's will has a lot to do with circumstances and timing. When the circumstances are right, when the time is right, don't be afraid to close. Know when to say, *"Il est fini."*

32 – OF PERSONAL PHILOSOPHY

It never ceases to amaze me how much we resemble each other, yet how different we all are. Some of us watch CNN; some of us watch FOX News. Some of us choose the evening news, or baseball, basketball, football, or whatever.

Your selection of which to watch probably depends on a biased viewpoint. You are not only a watcher, but also a thinker; which station you watch and which events you think about are matters of personal philosophy.

So, what is it about our mental makeup that determines our personal philosophy? It is, of course, a multitude of things: our upbringing, our education, our friends, our unique experiences.

At the time of this writing, President Obama has just fired four-star General Stanley McChrystal as commander of troops in Afghanistan. He fired him because of an article to appear in *Rolling Stone* magazine in which General McChrystal and his staff were reported to have bad-mouthed the president, the vice president, and the U.S. ambassador to Afghanistan. Obama did what he had to do to preserve military discipline. But why did McChrystal do what he did?

McChrystal followed his own personal philosophy. That doesn't make it acceptable, but that's what happened with the battle-hardened soldier. He knew the challenges he and his combat troops faced. His request for 40,000 additional troops had been delayed for months. He was fighting the war by killing people with deadly toy airplanes. His soldiers needed to ask permission from local Afghans to fire on the Taliban. Obama had asked for a meeting with McChrystal in Afghanistan. When he arrived, Obama was not prepared for the meeting. It was a photo op.

I think McChrystal believed the challenges he faced could not be overcome. I believe he felt the civilians directing the war didn't have a clue what they were doing. He wanted others to know what was going on. He even approved the article for *Rolling Stone* magazine before it was published. He had a strong personal philosophy and the firmness of his convictions.

Many of us have strong personal convictions about many things. But few of us have the firmness of those convictions. Firmness takes guts. Firmness takes courage. Sometimes our personal convictions fall short of justifying firm actions.

Personal philosophy is ours and ours alone. Nobody can provide it for us. It is something we have to develop and embrace on our own.

There is no systematic approach to personal philosophy. It just happens. Others may influence it. Learning may direct it. Circumstances may dictate it. But in the end, it is we who select it. Each of us tries to develop and decide on the basic principles of personal philosophy on which we live our lives. That all sounds good, but in reality, there are no principles. As Immanuel Kant wrote, "The business of philosophy is not to give rules, but to analyze the private judgments of common reason."

Traditional philosophy is not about rules. Traditional philosophy is a quest for rational understanding of basic fundamentals. Philosophy raises the most fundamental questions about the nature of understanding and knowledge.

There is an element of contradiction involved when people begin to think about philosophy. Philosophy involves the questioning of basic concepts, principles and methods of science, religion, and so forth. Philosophy is a quest for rational understanding of basics. Traditional philosophers seek, but may never know, the answers to some of our most important questions.

Personal philosophy is not like that. At the personal level, there is little time for most of us to think very long about anything. We act, for the most part, in accordance with our personal philosophy about how to choose what is best to do under a given set of circumstances. What principles do we live our lives upon? Each must evaluate those ourselves. A dear friend once told me, *"Live like you will live forever; live like you will die tomorrow."* I have found that to be good advice, so I try to plan and live my life that way.

Busy people don't have time to analyze reasons and rationales for everything they do. Instead, they rely on what is burned into them by life's teaching and experiences. What busy people do have time to do, on occasion, is to think about the basics. Are the basic values in our lives based on rational principles? If so, what are those rational principles? Is the way we believe and act still apropos?

Are you a religious person? If so, why? If not, why not? I am a religious person. I believe in God. My training has taught me to believe there is life after death. Life after death is not only possible, but probable. I believe that the soul travels after death according to whether it is diseased or healthy. *Strive to maintain a healthy soul.*

Where are your priorities? Can you properly balance work with home and loved ones? I strove my whole life to provide for my family. My job always came first because it was my responsibility to provide income for the family. I always had a job, but I was not particularly successful. My job failed to bring to me the honor I needed. I wish I could have done better. Instead of trying to be who I wanted to be, I should have tried to be who I was. *Don't try to be who you want to be. Be who you are.*

My immediate family came next. I have tried to love them in the best way I knew how. I wish I could have done better.

How do you view fairness? Do you demand justice, or do you forgive? I try to do both. *We must all live with the consequences of our actions;* and as we do, forgiveness is given.

How do you view knowledge and wisdom? Are the thoughts and experiences of those who came before you important to you? Do you consider yourself wise? Knowledge and understanding are of extreme importance to me. But despite all that knowledge and understanding, I am not a man of wisdom. I wish I was, but I am not. I have to try to figure things out in a rational manner. Since there is never enough time to do that, I sometimes wing it. I make emotional decisions. If I'm right, I'm right. If I'm wrong, I'm wrong. That's just the way it is. Most often, however, I try to take time to evaluate the knowledge available to me and rationalize what is best.

Are you liberal or conservative? Do you seek to change things, or are you a traditionalist? Is social justice important to you; and if so, how much are you willing to pay for it? How much responsibility do you feel toward your future offspring? I am slightly left of conservative. Nothing much matters to me except to have a coherent and loving family, a good job, a nice home, a few good friends, and, of course, health, security, and happiness.

How do you view responsibility? Today we live in an age where we can produce practically nothing for ourselves. What are you responsible for providing? What do you expect others to provide?

How do you find contentedness? What do you do to provide contentment for others? My view is that each of us must find our own contentment. Each of us must find our own happiness.

What are your boundaries? How far will you let others go? How far will you let yourself go? Most of us, at one time or another, must deal with those who try to take from us: try to take our jobs, our promotions, our loved ones, our respect. How far will you let them go? Will you muster the *courage for confrontation*, the *strength for forgiveness*, or as Plutarch suggested, *the wisdom to remain silent?* When possible, it's usually best to do as Theodore Roosevelt said: *"Speak softly and carry a big stick."*

The principles from which we choose our own personal philosophy reach back to the time of the early Greek philosophers. They haven't changed much. Often we must chose between conflicting principles. To do that, you must seek to "Know yourself." Are you a follower or a leader? Are you a worker or a talker? Are you of average or superior intellect? From where do you draw upon for faith to endure challenge and hardship?

What are your goals? Is happiness all that matters? Are consequences all that matter? Whatever they are, be ever true to self.

And finally, *what kind of legacy do you want to leave, and how do you want to be remembered?* A long ago, I decided the matters of legacy and remembrance. I wanted to leave somebody a lot of money, and I wanted to be remembered with honor. Well, guess what—I perceived that neither would happen. I never made a lot of money, and practically nobody treated me with honor. But legacy and remembrance are personal matters. Nobody cares about either except you, and sometimes your heirs. So I have changed my perception to believe I have made a lot of money and I was treated with honor. That works with legacy, but what about remembrance? Remember, we are all different. We all have different values. Sometimes we don't understand each other's views. Sometimes we do. How we are remembered is how we want to be remembered. Remember the importance of perception. It is perception that matters. It is perception of how we treat others, of how we speak, of how we perform. Each of us has to determine and act in the way we want to be remembered. I now know how I want to be remembered.

I want to be remembered as one of the billions of people on this earth who tried to do the best he could with what he had. It wasn't always easy, it wasn't always good, it wasn't always right, but I always tried to do the best I could—that's the way it was. And that is my wish for you.

Appendix A –
Bibliography And Suggested Reading

The Republic. Plato. Translated by Benjamin Jowett Translated by Benjamin Jowett. (Barnes and Noble Classics, 2004).

Basic Works of Aristotle. Aristotle. Richard McKeon, Editor. (Random House, Inc. 2001).

The Living Bible, Paraphrased. (Tyndale House Publishers, 1971).

The Prince. Niccolo Machiavelli. (Penguin Books, 1999).

The Supreme Philosophy of Man. Alfred Armand Montapert. (Books of Value, 1970).

The Elements of Moral Philosophy. James Rachels. (McGraw-Hill, 1994).

Public and Private Morality. Stuart Hampshire, Editor. (Cambridge University Press, 1991).

Political Thinking. Glen Tinder. (Longman Classics, 2003).

The Secret. Rhonda Byrne. (Atria Books, 2006).

Happiness. Richard Lavard. (Penguin Books, 2005).

The Five Love Languages. Gary Chapman. (Northfield Publishing, 2004).

The Untethered Soul. Michael A. Singer. (New Harbinger Publications, Inc, 2007).

A Companion to Ethics. Peter Singer, Editor. (Blackwell Publishing, 2005).

Happiness Is a Serious Problem. Dennis Prager. (Regan Books, 1999).

Quantum, A Guide for the Perplexed. Jim Al-Khalili. (Weidenfeld & Nicolson, 2003).

Relativity. Albert Einstein. Translated by Robert Lawson. (Barnes & Noble, 2004).

Wikipedia, the free encyclopedia. (www.Wikipedia.org).

On Contentedness of Mind. Plutarch. (Levenger Press, 2009).

The Story of Philosophy. Bryan Magee. (Dorling Kindersley, 2001).

Appendix B –
Selected Paraphrased Quotations

Paraphrased Quotations from

The Republic
By
Plato
Translated by Benjamin Jowett
Barnes and Noble Classics

- Right behavior is whatever those in power determine it to be.
- Leaders of the state are allowed to lie for the public good, but nobody else should meddle with it.
- The direction in which education starts a man will determine his future.
- There are four divisions of the soul: reason, the highest; understanding, the second; faith (or determination); and perception of shadows last.
- When a spirit of reverence enters a young man's soul, order is restored.
- Freedom creates more drones in the democratic state than in the oligarchical state.
- In the oligarchical (power in the hands of a few) state, drones are disqualified and driven from office, and therefore cannot train or gather strength. Whereas in a democracy, they are almost always the ruling power. The keener sorts speak and act, and the rest keep buzzing about the speakers' platform.
- The three primary classes of men are wisdom-loving, honor-loving, and profit-loving. Each will praise his own and deprecate the others.
- Reason, the very facility that is the very instrument of judgment, is not possessed by the covetous or ambitious man, but only by the philosopher.
- Nothing is pleasanter than health. But we don't know this is the greatest pleasure until we are ill.
- Mean employments are a reproach, because the individual is unable to control the creatures within him but has to court them, and his great study is how to flatter them.
- To be patient under suffering is best. Nothing is gained by impatience.

- When the dice have been thrown, order our affairs in the way that reason deems best, not like children who have had a fall. Banish the cry of sorrow by the healing heart.
- The soul that cannot be destroyed by an evil, whether inherent or external, must exist forever, and if existing forever, must be immortal.
- Education has two divisions, gymnastics for the body and music for the soul.
- When riches and virtue are placed together on the scales of balance, one always rises and the other falls.
- Lovers of grace and good rhythm depend on simplicity.

Paraphrased Quotations from

The Basic Works of Aristotle
**Edited By
Richard McKeon
Random House Inc.**

Politics

- The state is the highest form of community and aims at the highest good.
- Political rule aims primarily at the good of those who are ruled. Democracy is the rule of the poor. Oligarchy is rule of the rich. But both sides miss the true object of the state, which is virtue.
- Justice is not the will of the majority or the wealthy, but the course of action that the moral aim of the state requires.
- A citizen is one who possesses political power. A good citizen knows both how to rule and how to obey.

Nichomachean Ethics

- The chief good is that which all things aim at.
- The highest of all good is happiness. For some, other high goods include pleasure, wealth, or honor.
- In the case of the multitudes of men, the things they individually esteem pleasant often clash.
- Workings in the way of virtue are what determine happiness.
- Excellence in man is divided into two classes: Intellectual and Moral.
- Moral choice seems to be those things that are in our own power.
- The most distinguishing characteristic of a good man is his seeing of the truth in every instance.
- He is brave who withstands and fears, and is bold, in respect of right objectives, from a right motive, in right manner, and at right times.
- Meekness is praised. The meek man is not led away by passions.
- The Soul attains truth from Art, Knowledge, Practical Wisdom, Science, and Intuition.
- A man who is good at deliberation will be practically wise.

- We should execute speedily what has been resolved upon deliberation, but deliberate slowly.
- Bodily pleasure drives out pain, and because pain is felt in excess, men pursue pleasure in excess.
- A good man prefers a brief and great joy to a tame and enduring one, and one great and noble action to many trifling ones.

Paraphrased Quotations from

The Prince
By
Niccolo Machiavelli
Penguin Books

- An unarmed prophet will have his career end in disaster.
- Qualities considered virtuous in a Christian are not virtuous in a prince.
- All politicians are doomed to failure some of the time.
- Support weaker powers without increasing their strength. Crush the powerful.
- Whoever is responsible for another becoming powerful ruins himself.
- A wise prince should rely on what he controls, not on what he cannot control.
- Violence must be inflicted once for all; people will then forget what it tastes like and so be less resentful.
- To those seeing him, a price should appear to be a man of compassion, a man of good faith, a man of integrity, a kind and gentle man.
- People are always impressed by appearance and results.
- A prince should avoid anything that will make him hated and despised.
- Princes should delegate to others the enactment of unpopular measures and keep in their own hands the means of winning favors.
- Above all, a prince must endeavor to win the reputation of being a great man of outstanding ability.
- A prince wins prestige for being a true friend or a true enemy. If you do not declare yourself, you will always be at the mercy of the conqueror. The conqueror does not want doubtful friends. The loser repudiates you because you were unwilling to throw your lot with him. When you boldly declare your support for one side, if that side conquers, he is under obligation to you.
  If your ally is defeated, he will shelter you and will help you while he can, and you will become associates whose joint fortunes may well change for the better.

- Never join in an aggressive alliance with someone more powerful than you, unless it is a matter of necessity.
- A prince should show his esteem for talent, actively encouraging able men and honoring those who excel in their profession.
- If a man behaves with patience and circumspection and the time and circumstances are such that the method is called for, he will prosper. But if circumstances change, he will be ruined if he does not change his policy.
- Fortune is changeable, whereas men are obstinate in their ways. Men prosper so long as fortune and policy are in accord, and when there is a clash, they fail.

Paraphrased Quotations from

The Supreme Philosophy of Man
By
Alfred Armand Montapert
Books of Value

- You become what you dwell upon.
- Don't fight nature; use it, and cooperate with it.
- You are happiest when you are doing something you like and something you are good at.
- We are being educated to depend on each other for almost everything.
- Give your decisions, never your reasons; your reasons may be right, your reasons may be wrong.
- The first lesson in the art of living is to distinguish the important from the unimportant.
- Envy is a deadly disease.
- Bad habits can ruin the entire life of a person.
- Develop strength to overcome the vicissitudes (unexpected changes) of life.
- The time to count your friends is in the day of adversity.
- There is no explanation quite so effective as silence. If you are right, your life will do its own explaining.
- Our first responsibility in life is to take care of ourselves.
- All men are unequal. They were born unequal.
- Simplify your life.
- Good mental health means you are able to get along with yourself. You are able to get along with others. You are able to get along with circumstances.
- Three steps to enjoying a healthy mind are: 1) control anger and passions of the mind, 2) the conquest of fear, and 3) the elimination of worry.
- There is one thing over which each person has absolute, inherent control—their mental attitude. No one can hurt you except yourself.
- There are many things in life that everyone needs to remember; and there are just as many things that everyone needs to forget.

- Most men whose work brings them in contact with the general public have learned that the ability to remember names and faces and personal incidents is a real asset.
- To improve your memory, practice this: 1) Make a conscious effort to remember, 2) Be sure you understand the meaning of what you want to remember, 3) Use a trick, and 4) Become interested in what you want to remember.

Political Thinking
By
Glenn Tinder
Longman Classics

Instructions in the art of thinking:
- Do not try to arrive at ideas no one has ever thought of before.
- Be open.
- Do not hurry.
- Make plenty of notes.
- Be aware of substituting reading for thinking.

Basic concepts:
- Conservative—Human beings are selfish and competitive.
- Liberal—Human beings are for the most part rational.
- The idea that human beings are equal means they are equal only in their rights before the law. They are clearly not equal in intelligence or health or emotional balance.
- Serious mistakes can be made when reliance is placed in masses of ordinary people who lack the time, training, information, and all else needed for making accurate judgments.
- There are absolutely superior human beings. The only ones who can identify them are others of like superiority.
- Competition automatically sifts out the superior people.
- How much of your time is politics worth?
- Politics is likely to repel sensitive and honorable people and attract the insensitive and unscrupulous.
- There is no way of avoiding it: a political system is essentially a set of arrangements by which some people dominate others.
- Tradition is fragile and irreplaceable. It can be destroyed through reckless technological and social change and cannot, once destroyed, be easily rebuilt.
- Traditions practically always embody marked inequalities.
- Discovery of the truth is difficult, even for the greatest of minds, and beyond the capacity of average minds.
- Scientists and philosophers had primary responsibility for finding the truth and for making it known.
- Man and society are shaped primarily by economic relationships.

- We cannot control the course of history. History is seen as a product of economic necessity rather than human ideas and intentions. Human beings thus have little control over the course of events.
- Change is the very essence of reality.

Paraphrased Quotations from

The Secret
by
Rhonda Byrne
Atria Books

- You can have anything you want: happiness, health, and wealth.
- The secret is the law of attraction. Everything that is coming into your life, you are attracting into your life. You are a magnet.
- Hold onto the thoughts of what you want. Meditate daily. Repeat: "I am master of my own mind." Say it often.
- We have about sixty thousand thoughts a day. Shifters are things that change your feelings in a snap: things like beautiful memories, future events, funny moments, nature, a person you love, your favorite music.
- The feeling of love is the highest frequency you can emit.
- Turn every life situation into a positive one.
- In the morning, think in advance the way you want to go.
- In the evening, think through the events of the day. If any moments did not go the way you wanted, replay them in your mind in the way that thrills you.
- Make a list of the things to be grateful for. Say "thank you" hundreds of times. Set your thoughts and frequency on happiness.
- Love and gratitude will dissolve all negativity in our lives.
- Stress is one of the worst things you can do when you're trying to heal yourself.
- Think thoughts of perfection. Science shows we will have a brand-new body in a very short time. Know your body is only months old.
- When people completely focus on what's wrong and their symptoms, they will perpetuate it. Healing will not occur until attention is shifted from being sick to being well.
- Happiness is a state of being. Push the happy button.
- You cannot help the world by focusing on negative things.
- Praise and bless everything in your life. Use praise to bring forth health, wealth, and happiness.

- There is a "wow" factor when you think about what you want. You emit a frequency. You cause the energy of what you want to vibrate at that frequency and bring it to you.
- You have to get competition out of your mind, and become a creative mind. Focus only on your visions, and take all competition out of the equation.

Paraphrased Quotations from

The Untethered Soul
By
Michael A. Singer
New Harbinger Publications, Inc.

- You have a mental dialogue going on inside your head all the time. Step back and examine this voice. Notice the voice takes both sides of the conversation.
- Consciousness has the ability to selectively focus on specific objects.
- Every emotion you have, every thought that passes your mind is an expenditure of energy.
- Just stop telling your mind that it is your job to fix your personal life. Your mind has very little control over this world.
- Relax your heart until you are face-to-face with the exact place where it hurts. Then relax. Keep relaxing. Relax your shoulders and relax your heart. Let go and give room for the pain to pass though you. Dare to face the pain, and it will pass.
- The only reason you don't feel energy all the time is because you block it. You block it by closing your heart, closing your soul.
- The only thing you really want from life is to feel enthusiasm, joy, and love.
- Your heart, your soul, is an energy center. The heart, the soul, becomes blocked by stored unfinished energy patterns from the past.
- Unfinished energy patterns end up ruining your life. Stored blockages, impressions from the past, sometimes get activated years later.
- When old energies come back up because you were unable to process them before, let them go now. Just open, relax your heart, forgive, laugh, or do anything you want. Don't just push them back down.
- Just have fun experiencing whatever happens next. Go about your business and put yourself at ease. There is tremendous joy, beauty, love, and peace within you. Just accept that it is there and that you are going to feel it.
- When you are comfortable with pain passing through you, you will be free.

- If you want to be happy, you have to let go of the part of your heart that wants to create melodrama.
- You don't want your happiness to be conditional upon other people.
- Life is giving you a gift. That gift is the flow of events that takes place between your birth and your death.
- Death is the great equalizer. Anytime you're having trouble with something, think of death.

Paraphrased Quotations from

The Five Love Languages
By
Gary Chapman
Northfield Publishing

- Your emotional love language and the love language of your spouse are different. We must learn our spouse's primary love language.
- There are five basic love languages: Words of Affirmation, Quality Time, Receiving Gifts, Acts of Service, and Physical Touch.
- The need to feel loved is a primary emotional need, a sense that one is wanted and belongs.
- A person who is in love has the illusion that his beloved is perfect. Falling in love is not an act of will or a conscious choice. We cannot make it happen.
- Sometimes our words are saying one thing, but our tone of voice is saying another. Our spouses will usually interpret our message based on the tone of our voice, not the words we use.
- It's not what you say, but the way you say it.
- A soft answer turns away anger.
- Love doesn't keep a score of wrongs. Love doesn't bring up past failures.
- The best thing you can do with failures of the past is to let them be history.
- Choose to live today free from the failures of yesterday.
- Love makes requests, not demands.
- The deepest human need is the need to feel appreciated.
- We must be willing to give advice, but only when requested and never in a condescending manner.
- Most of us have very little training in listening. When listening, try to: maintain eye contact when your spouse is talking, don't listen to your spouse and do something else at the same time, listen for feelings, observe body language, ask for clarification, and refuse to interrupt.
- People tend to criticize their spouse most loudly in the area where they themselves have the deepest emotional need.

- Ask your spouse to make a list of ten things he or she would like you to do during the next month. Ask your spouse to prioritize them by numbering from 1 to 10.
- The most important thing you can do for your mate in a time of crisis is to love him or her. Hug and kiss your spouse.
- Observe your children. Watch how they express love to others. That is a clue to their love language.

Paraphrased Quotations from

On Contentedness of Mind
By
Plutarch
Levenger Press

- Wine compels a prudent man to say what is best left unsaid. If anyone pledge you to drink with him at a dinner when you have had enough, do not be bashful, do not do violence to nature, but put the cup down without drinking. Keep the tongue under control.
- Talkativeness is a disease very difficult to control. Its remedy requires hearers; but talkative people hear nobody.
- A word once spoken cannot be recalled. Those who have enjoyed a truly noble and royal education learn first to be silent and then to speak.
- Silence is the answer to wise men. Silence never brings pain or sorrow. Nothing is more highly thought of than silence.
- The desire to know other people's troubles is a disease harmful and brings storm and darkness to the soul.
- Envy is pain at another's blessings, and malignity at another's misfortunes. Both proceed from the same vice, ill-nature.
- Fits of anger, that gather together in the soul by degrees, are generated within us by selfishness and peevishness. The first way to overcome anger is not to obey or listen when it bids you to speak loud.
- Strive to remove anger by not forbidding those who are to be corrected to speak in their defense, but by listening to them.
- It is impossible to check irresponsible power, unless one wields power with much meekness.
- Nothing causes us to be mild to our servants and wives and friends as much as easiness and simplicity and learning to be content with what we have.
- Neither marriage nor friendship is bearable with anger.
- A prudent man should commit nothing to fortune, nor neglect anything.
- Events will take their course, it is no good our being angry with them, he is happiest who wisely turns them to the best account.

- If you take people as they are, you will be happier in the disposition you will then have.
- All things are not within anyone's power, and we must obey *Know thyself,* and adapt ourselves to our natural bent.
- The sensible person hopes for better things, but expects worse, and makes the most of either.
- He who understands the nature of the soul has, in his fearlessness of death, no small help to ease of mind in life.
- Remember the past with thankfulness, and meet the future without fear.

Appendix C –
Suggested Discussion Questions

1. How much of this book did you read?
2. Which chapters did you not read? Why?
3. Of the chapters you read, which did you find the most interesting? The most thought provoking? The most agreed with? The most disagreed with?
4. We all think differently. We all have different values. When, if ever, are you comfortable talking with those who have slightly different values from yours? With moderately different values from yours? With values directly opposite from yours? Why?
5. It has often been said, "Never talk about politics or religion." When are you comfortable talking about politics and religion? When are you not comfortable? Why?
6. Has your personal philosophy changed during your lifetime? What caused it to change?
7. Most all of us have experienced great personal happiness and great tragedy. How do you deal with great personal happiness? How do you deal with great personal tragedy? How do you deal with the happiness and tragedy of others?
8. What does success mean to you? What does failure mean to you?
9. Does scientific knowledge enter into your religion? In what way?
10. Which professions do you most admire? Which do you least admire?
11. Are you mostly a rational person or an emotional person? When do you rely on faith?

Author's Note:
Feel free to contact the author with questions and comments, and for telephone interviews. The author's 2010 e-mail address is:
norm315@msn.com